COLOR YOUR WORLD

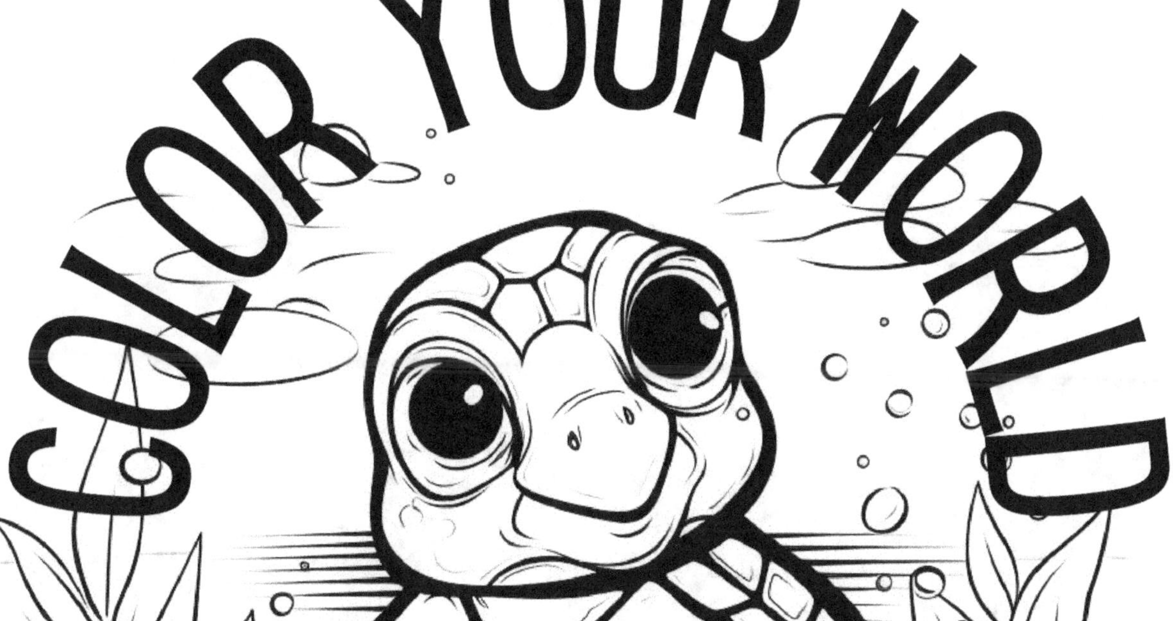

Nic Essary & Cody Essary

80 Page Coloring Book

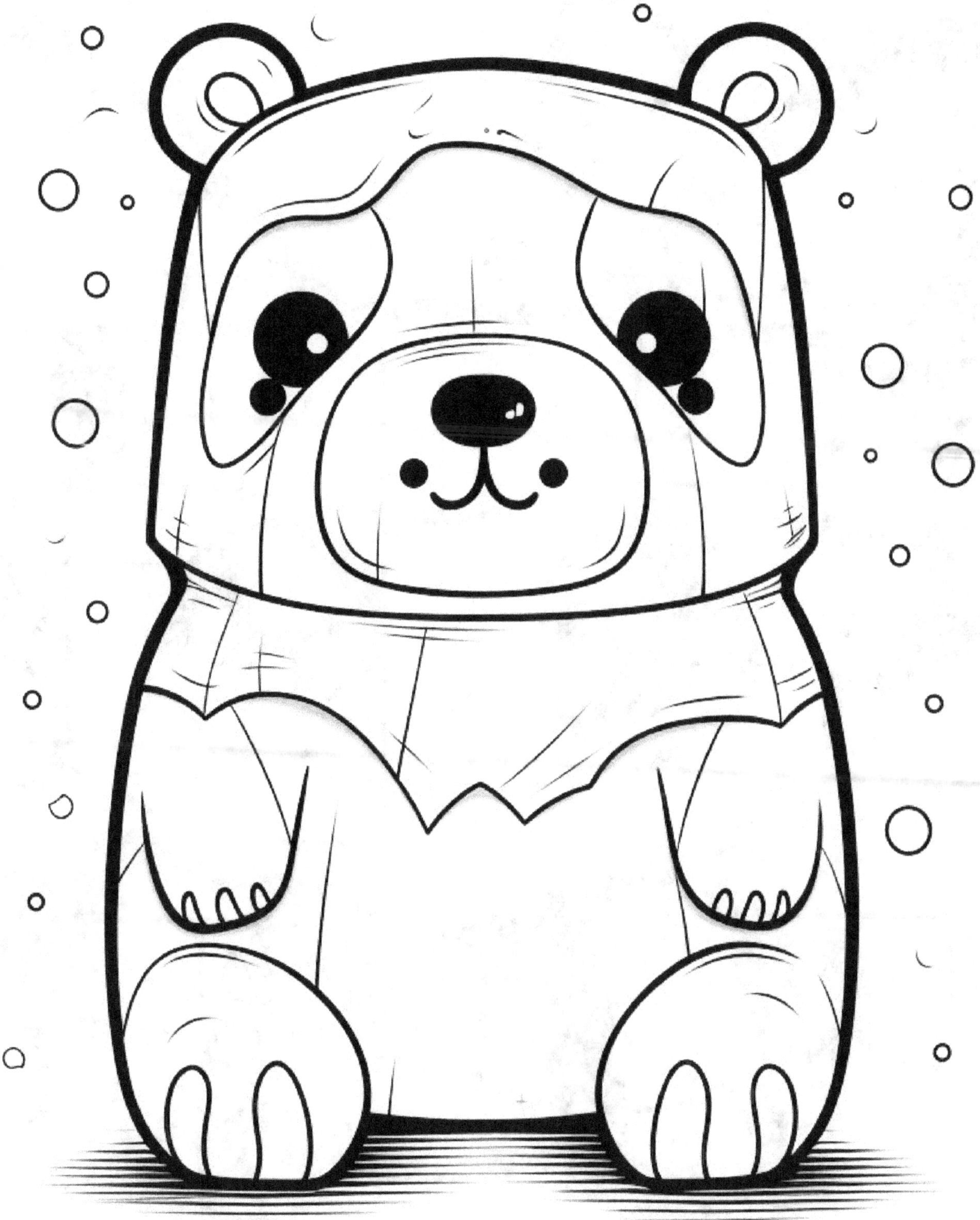

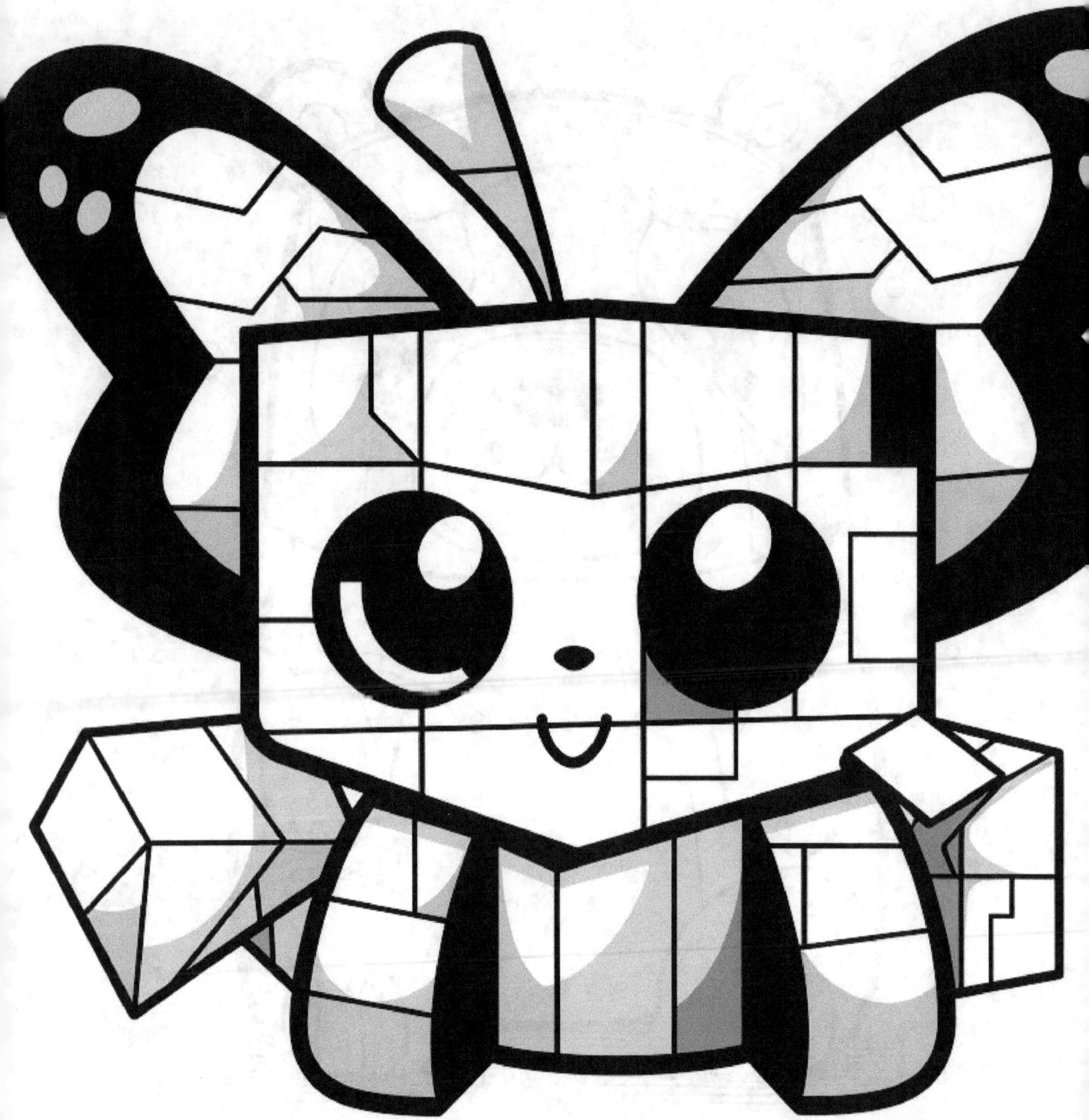

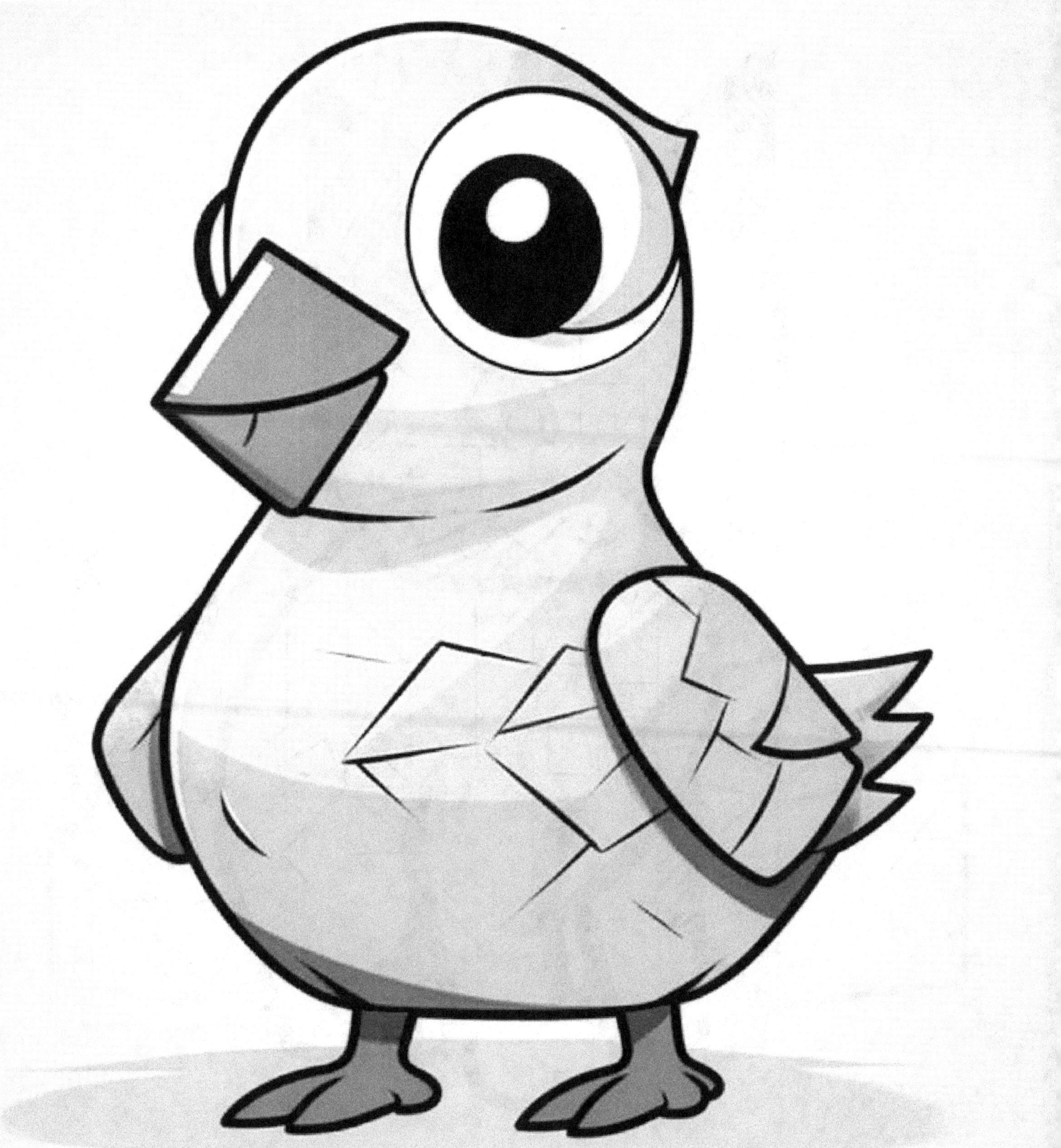

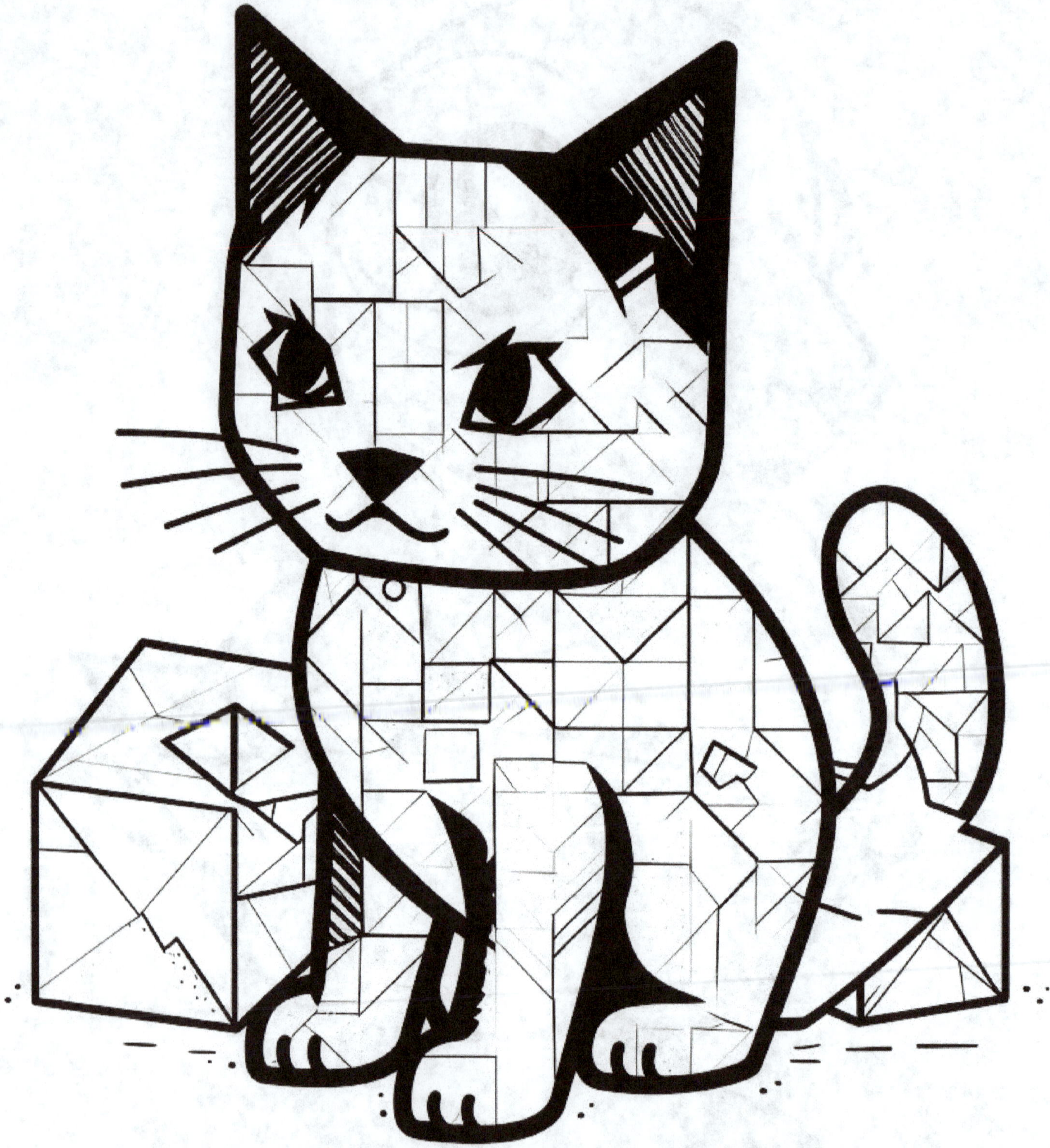

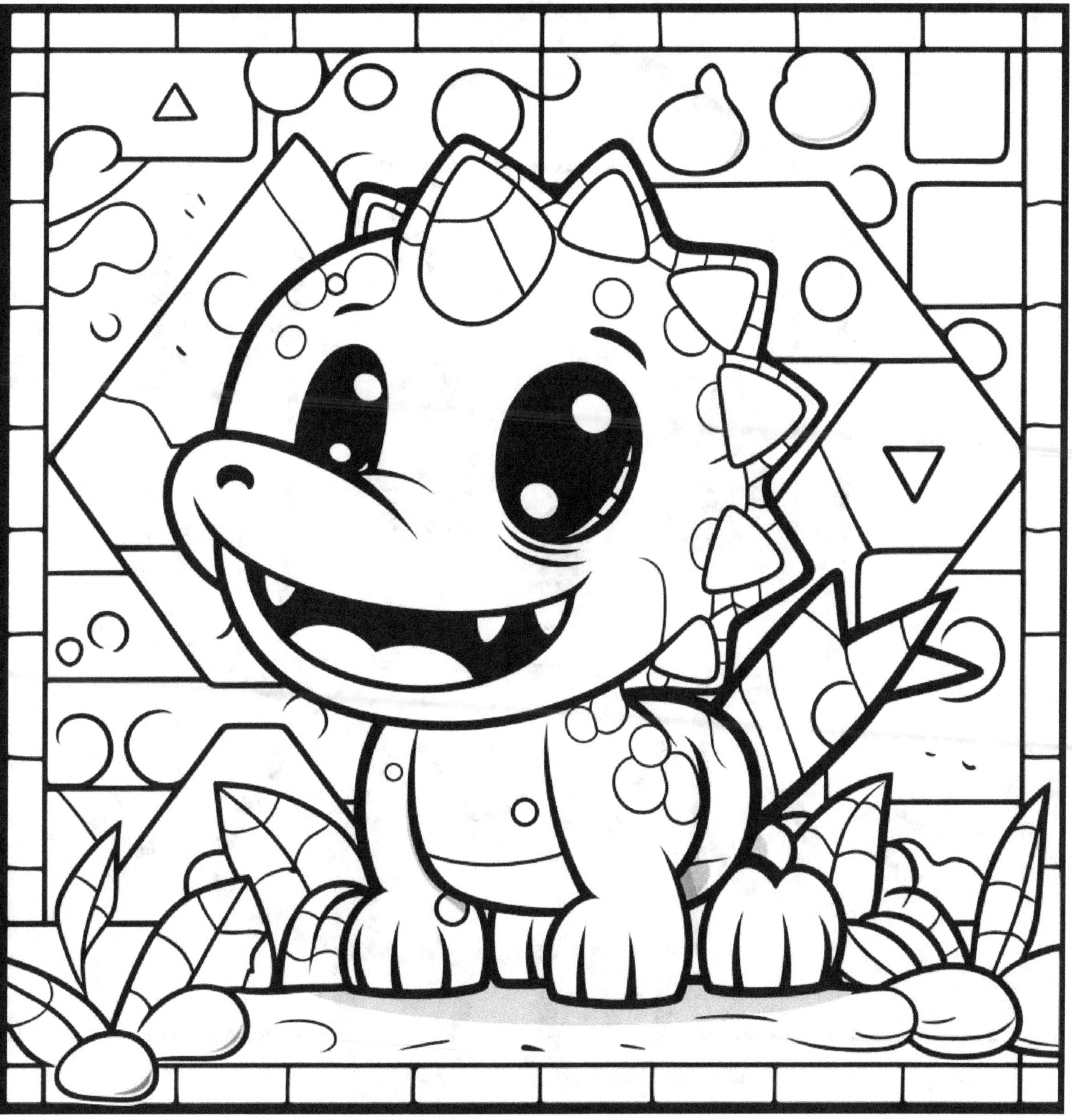

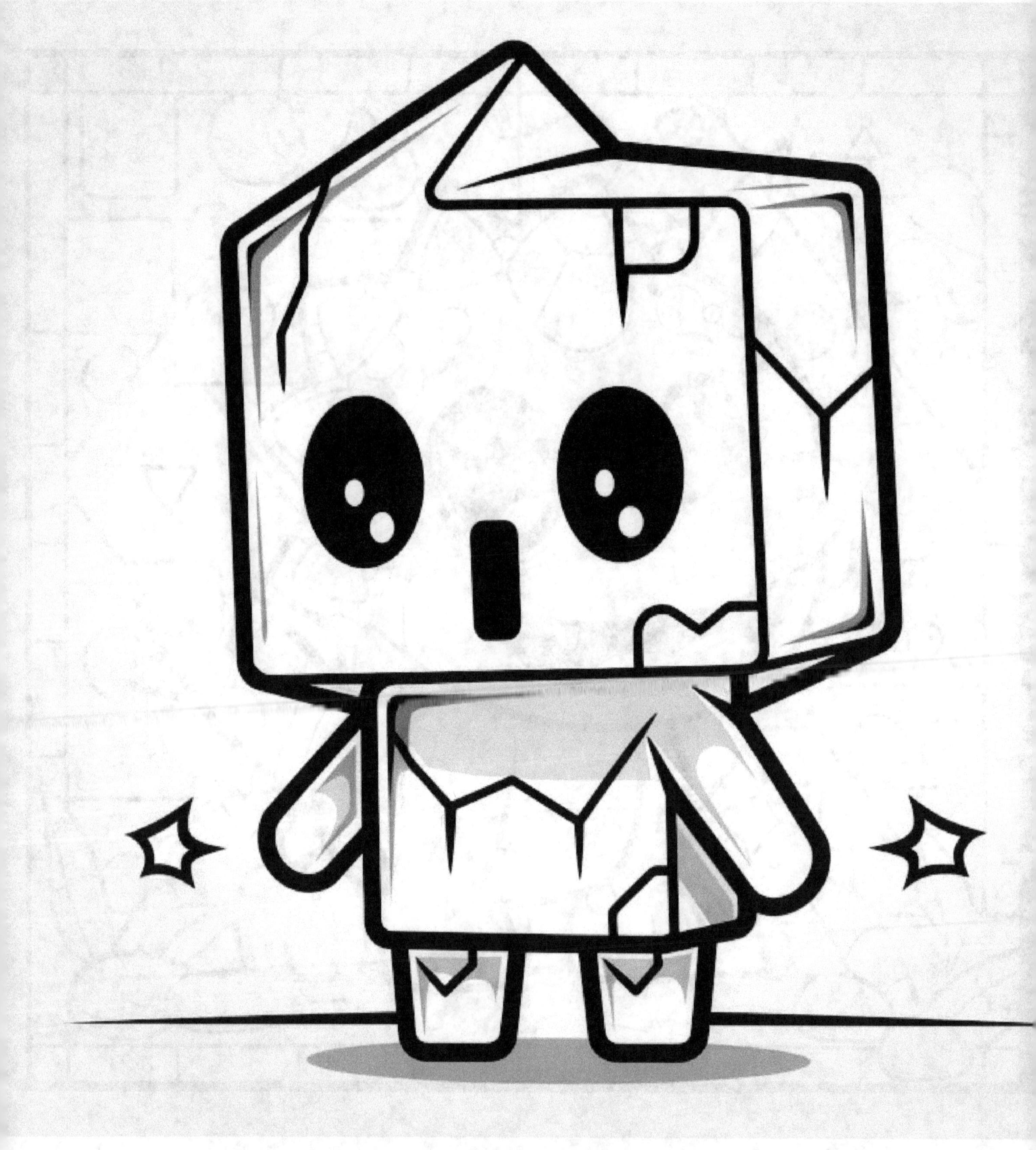

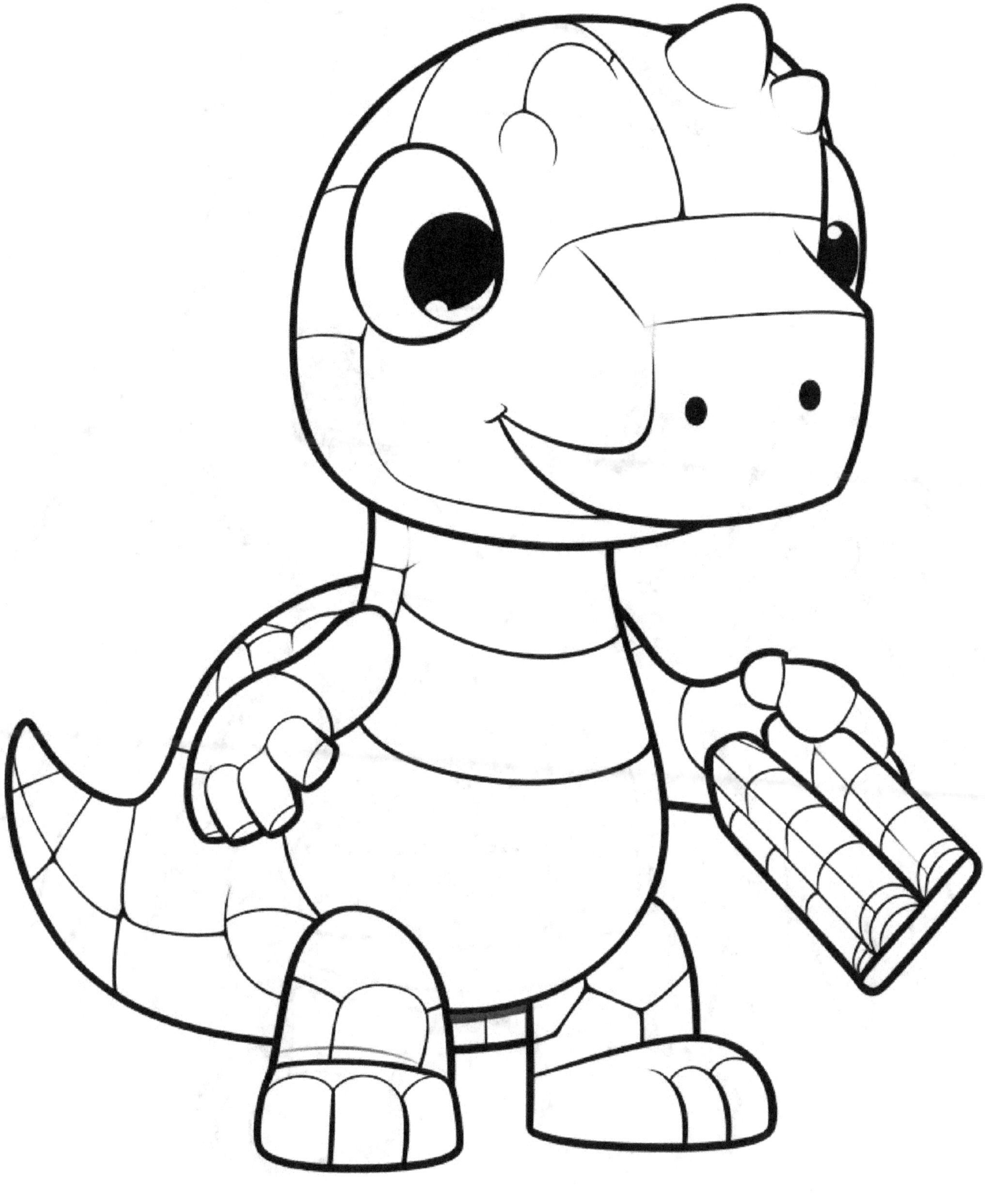

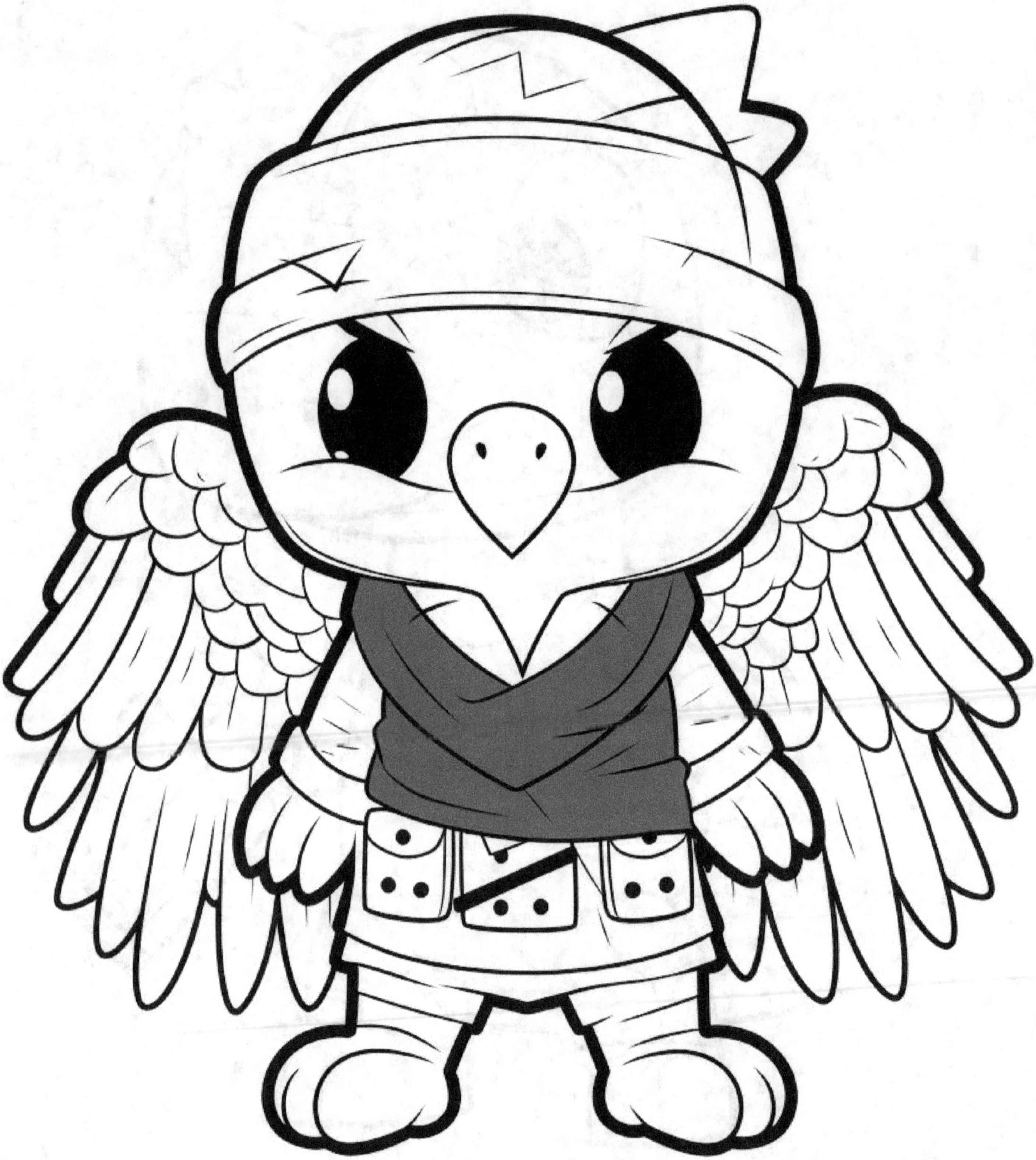

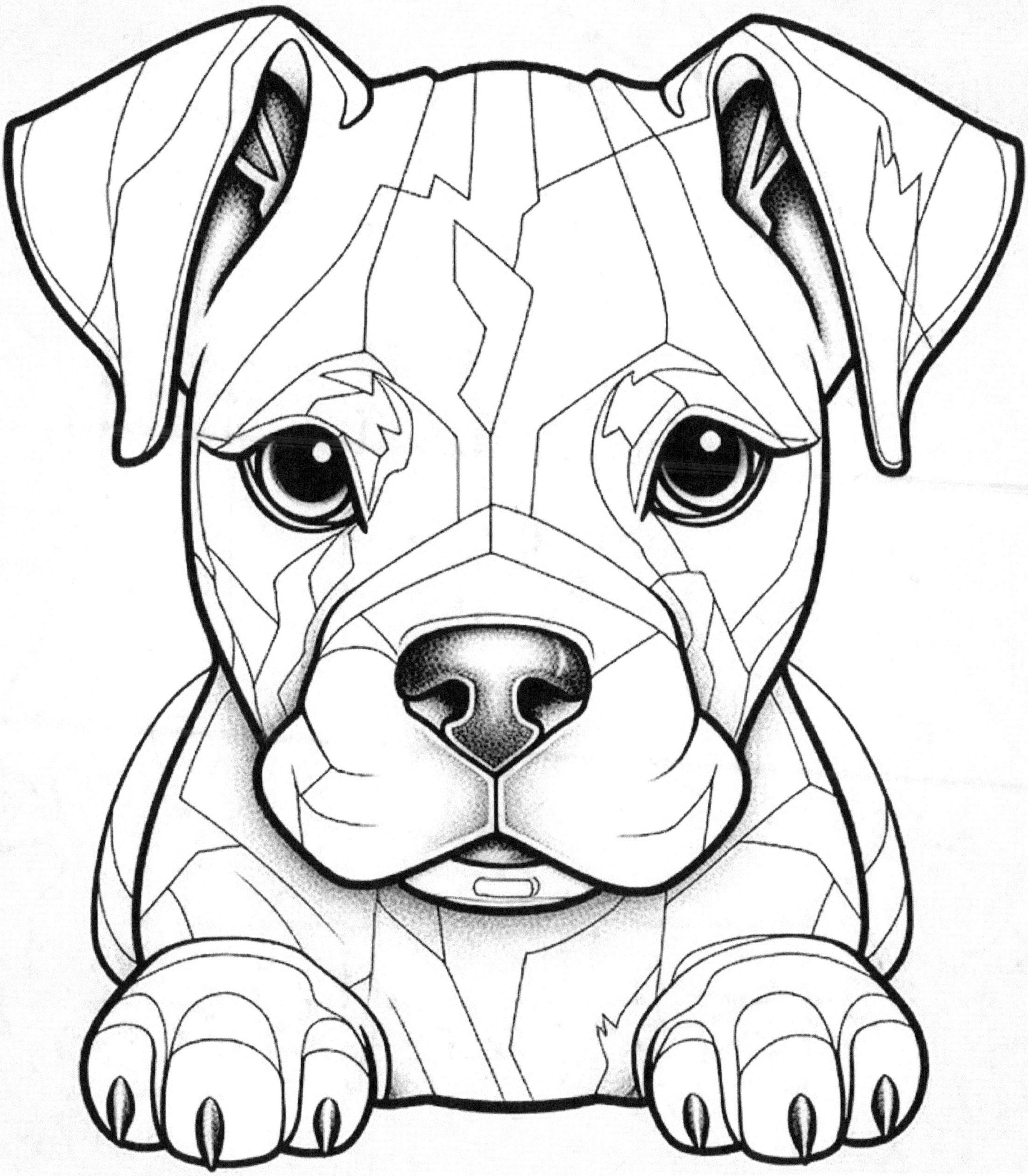

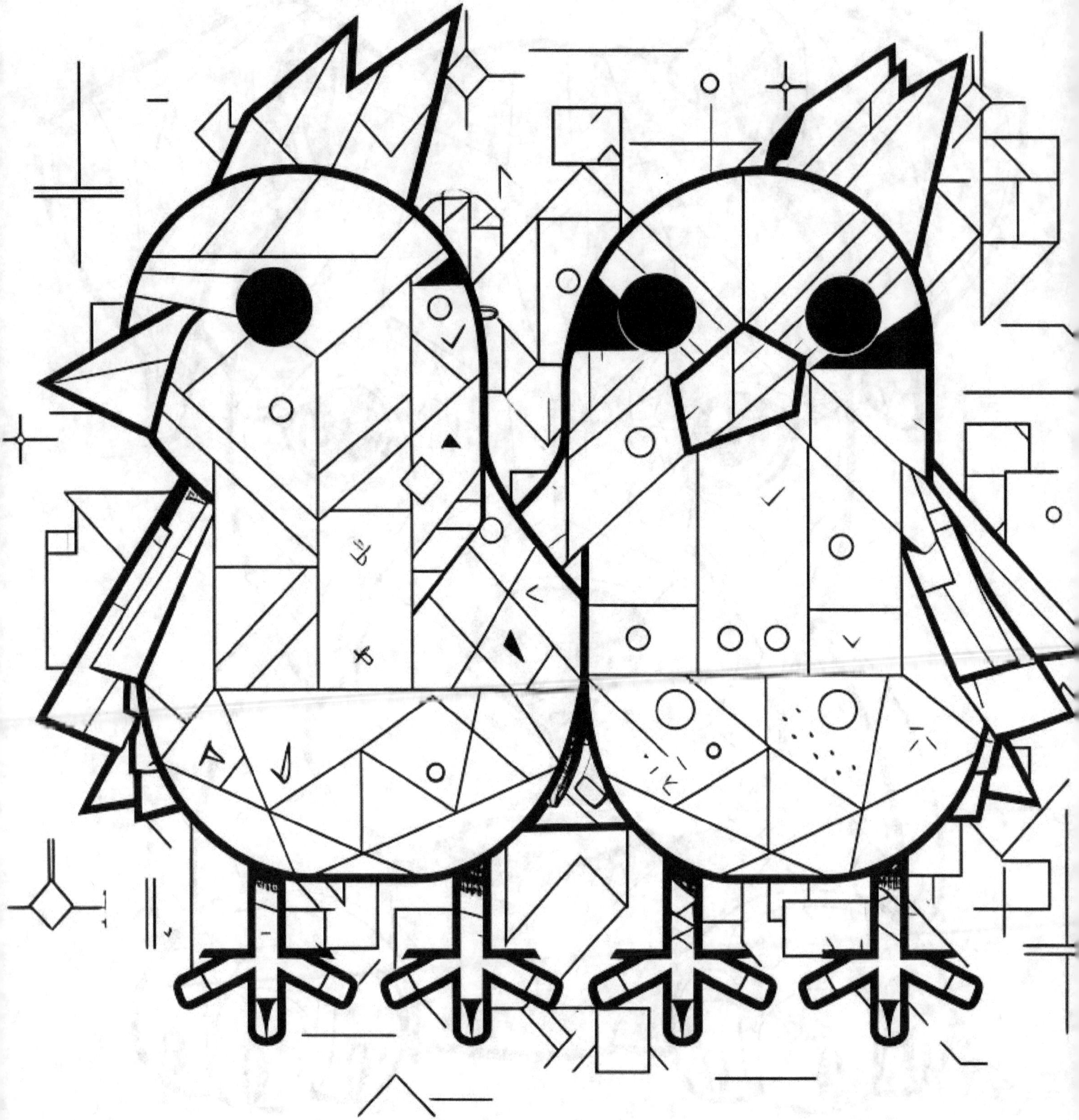

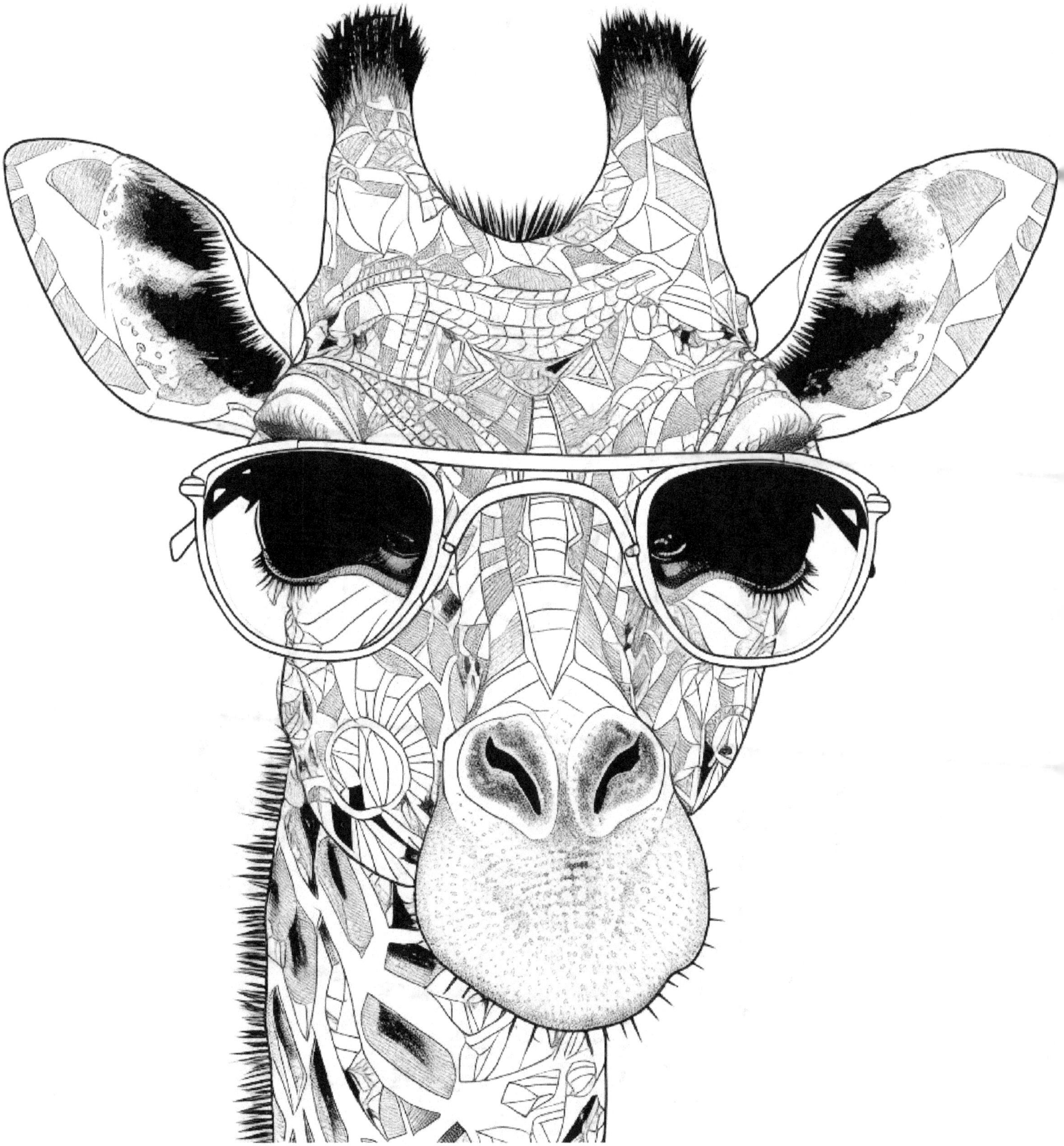

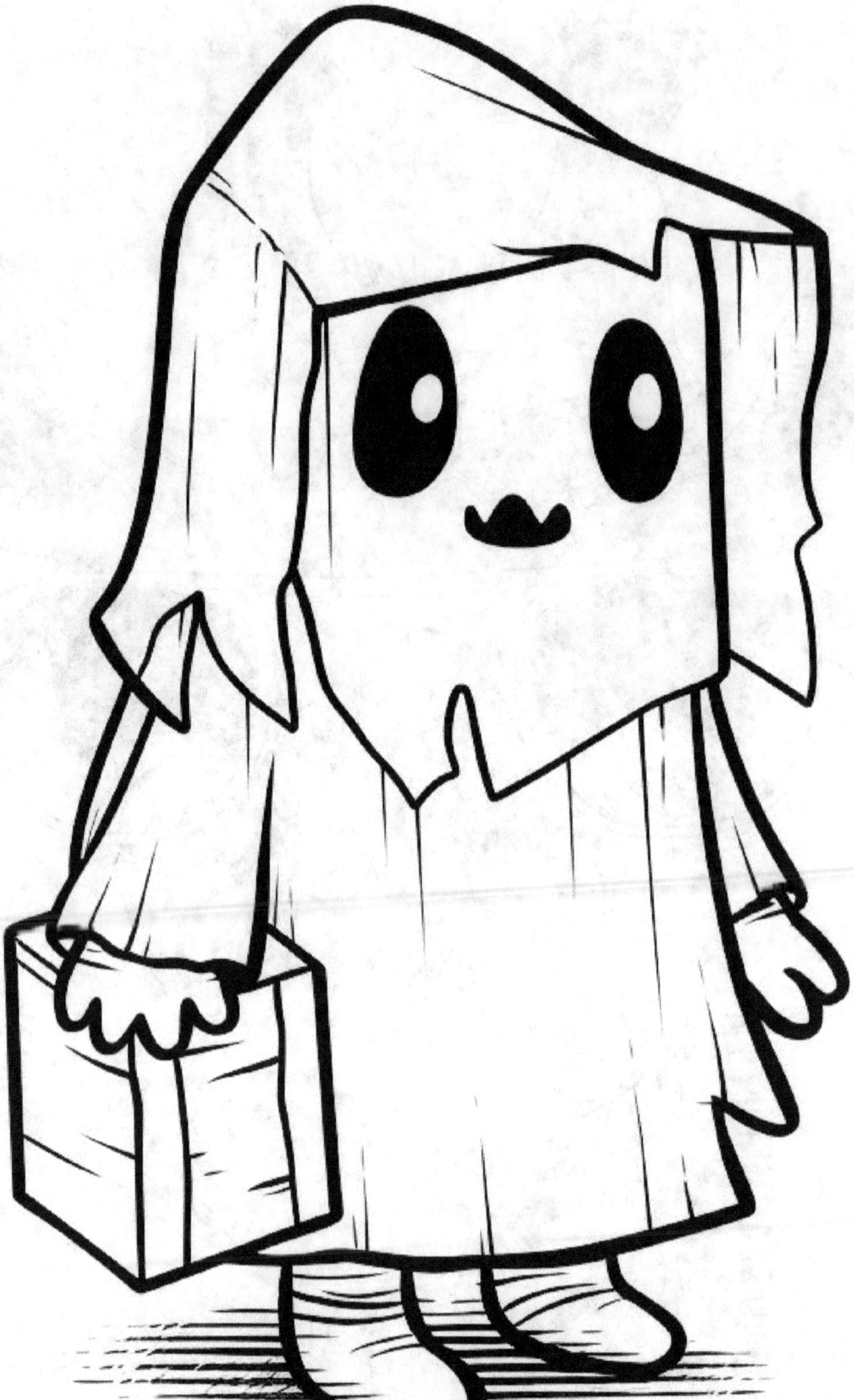

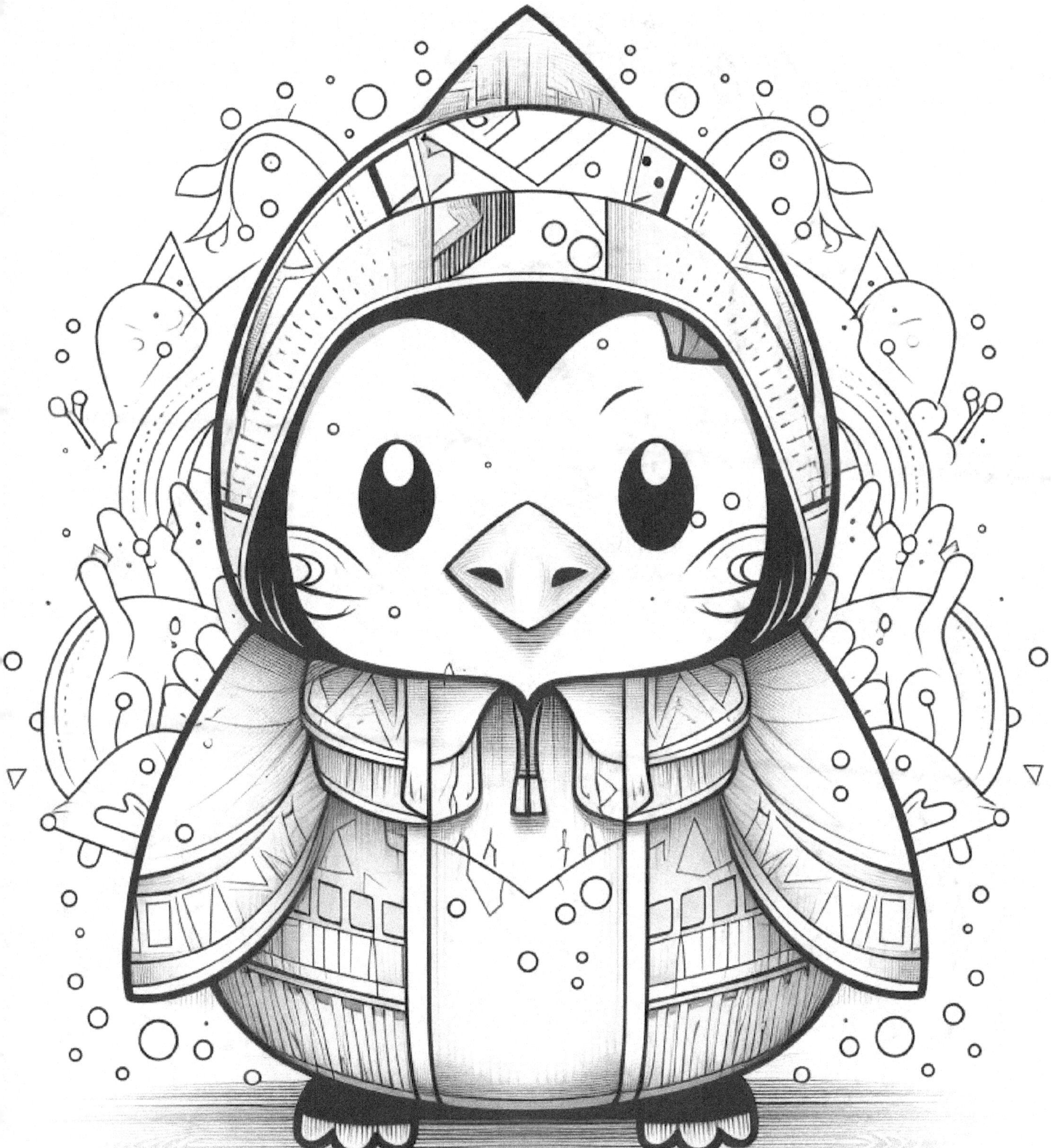

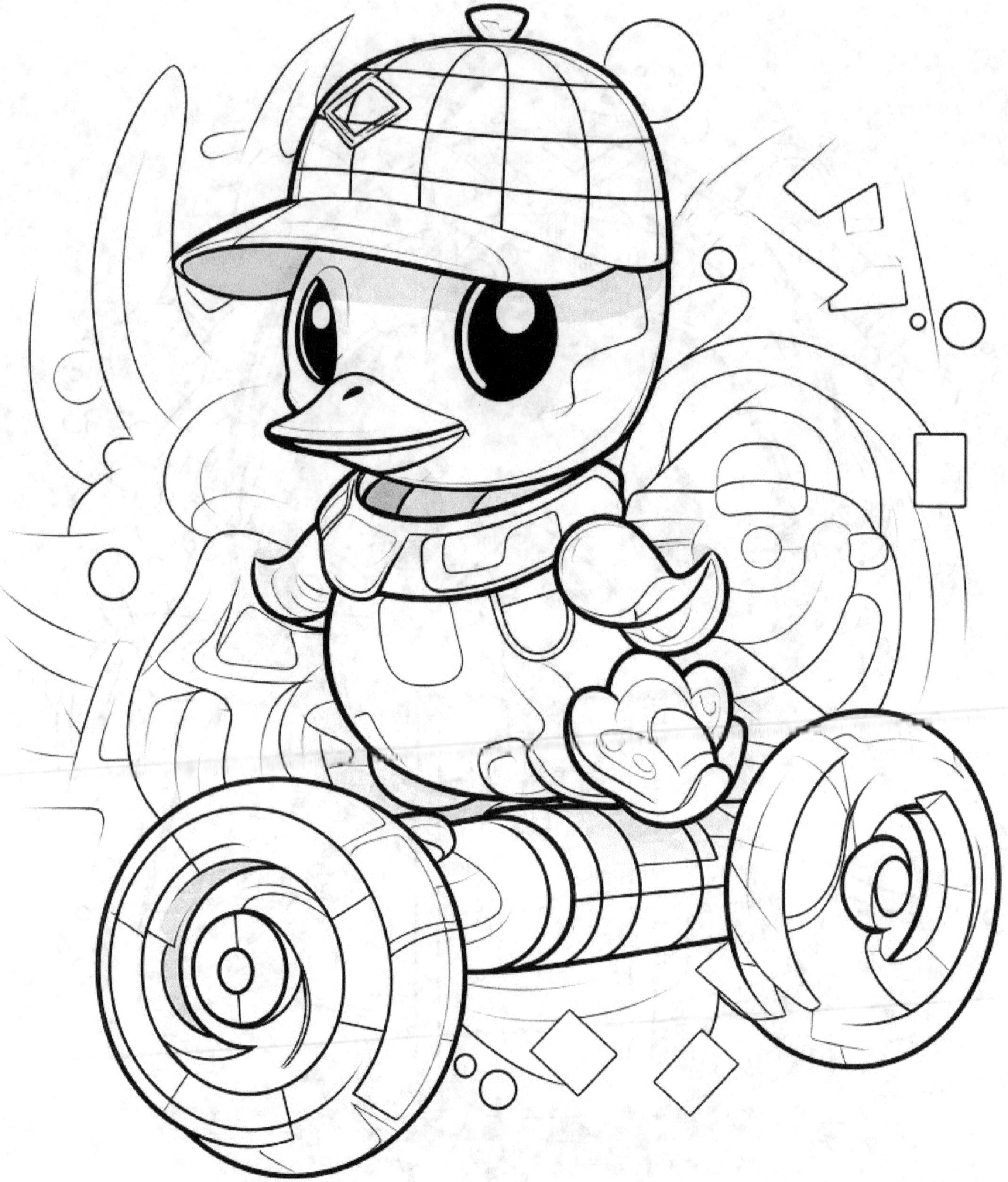

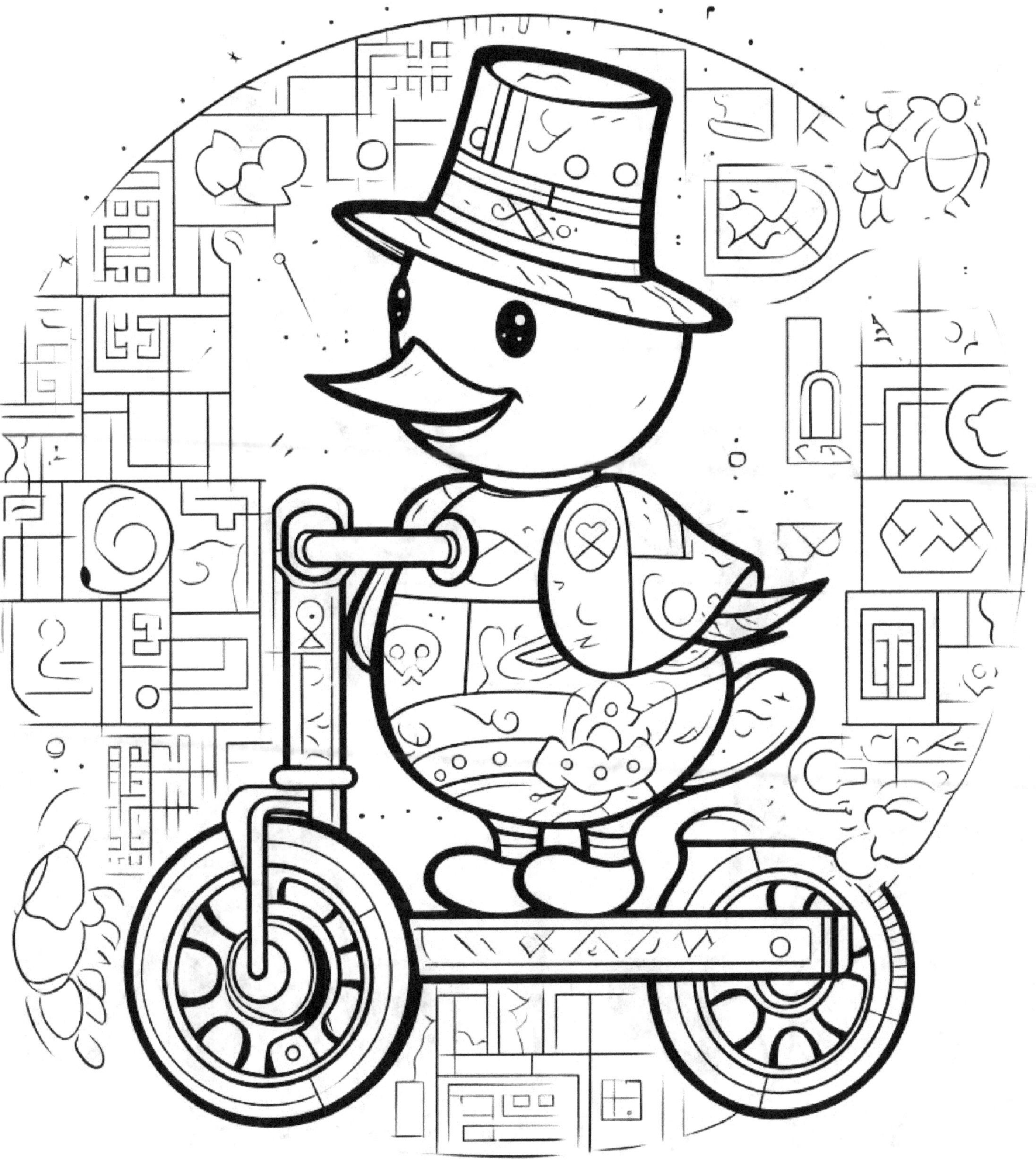

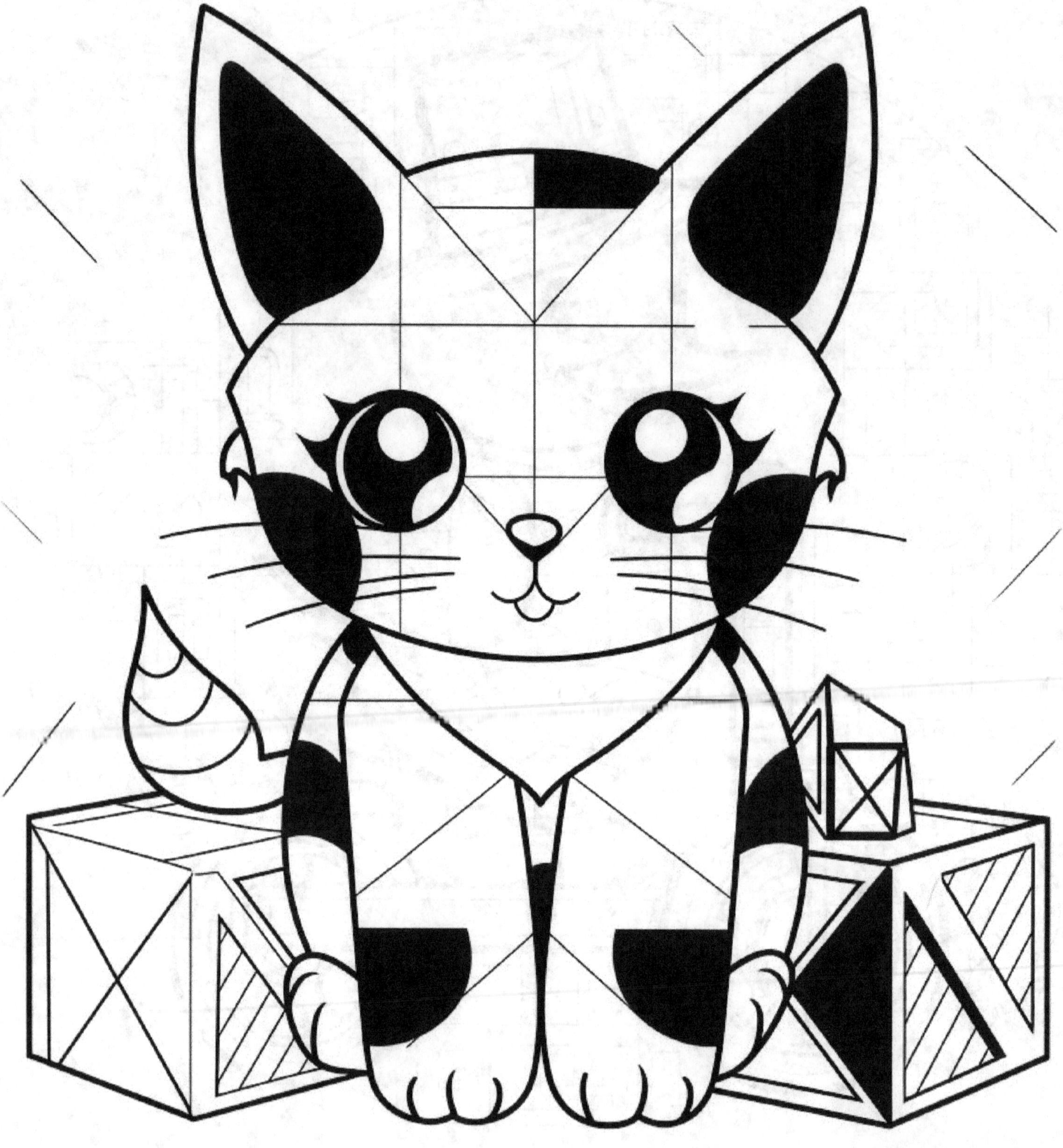

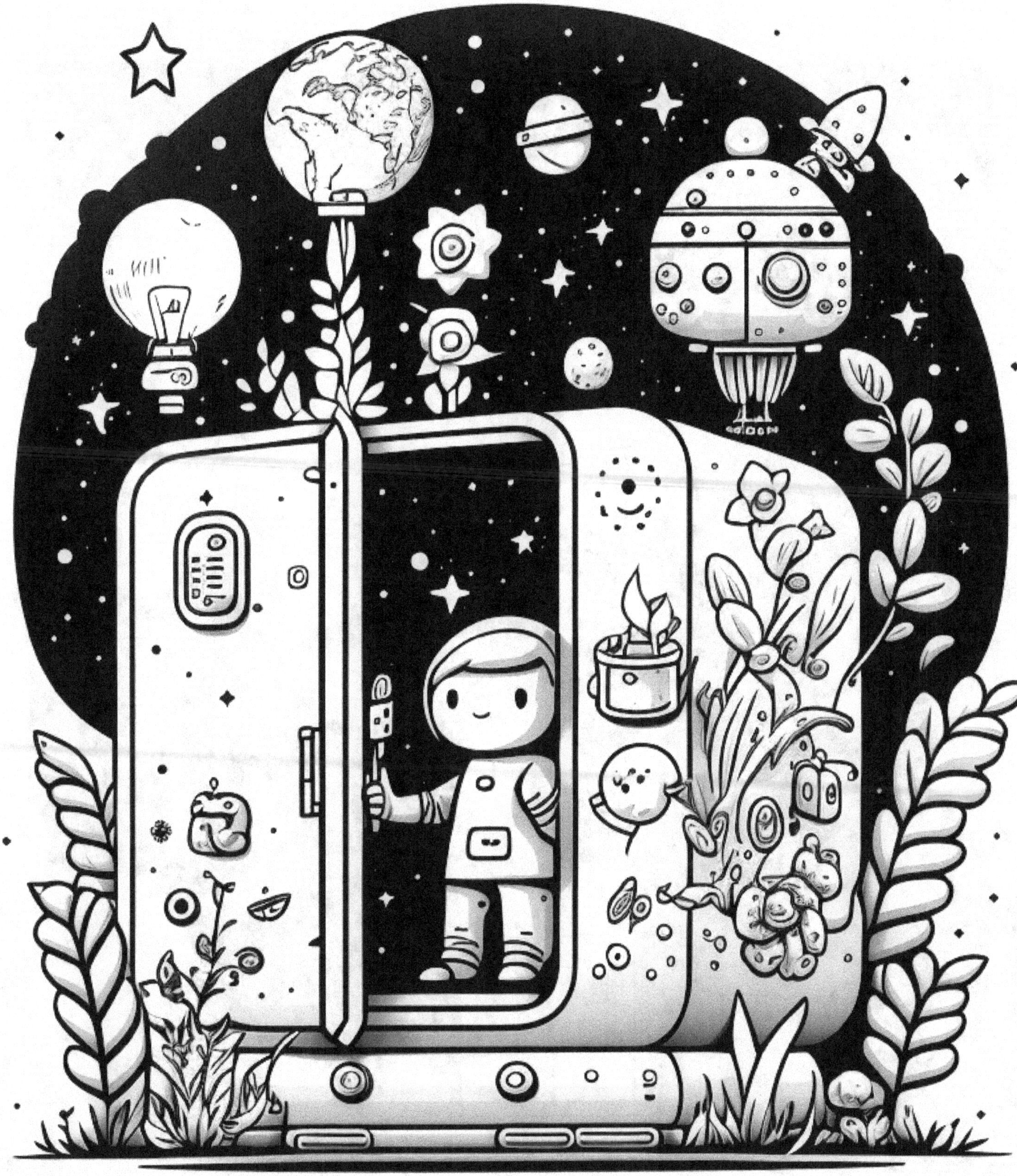

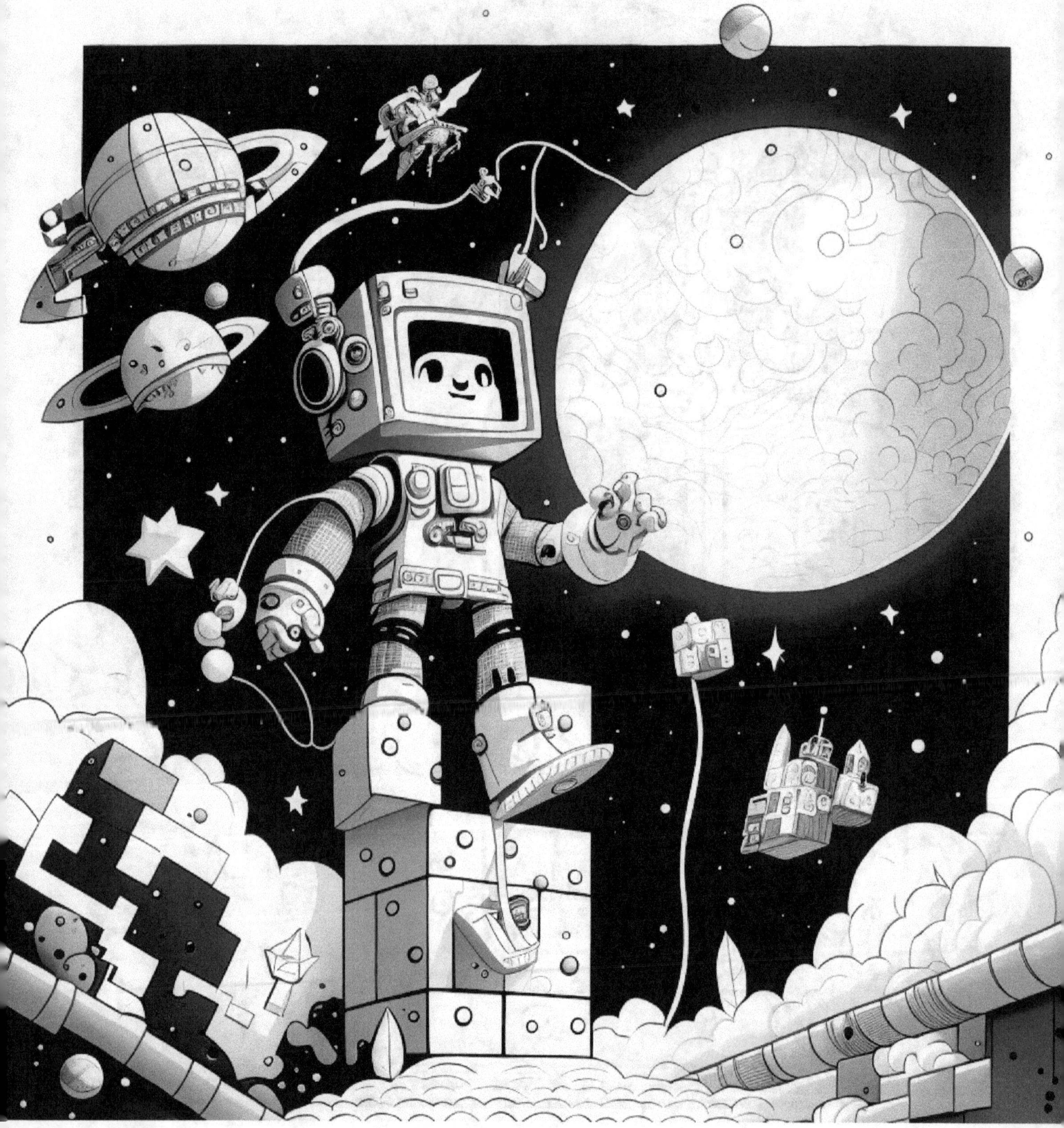

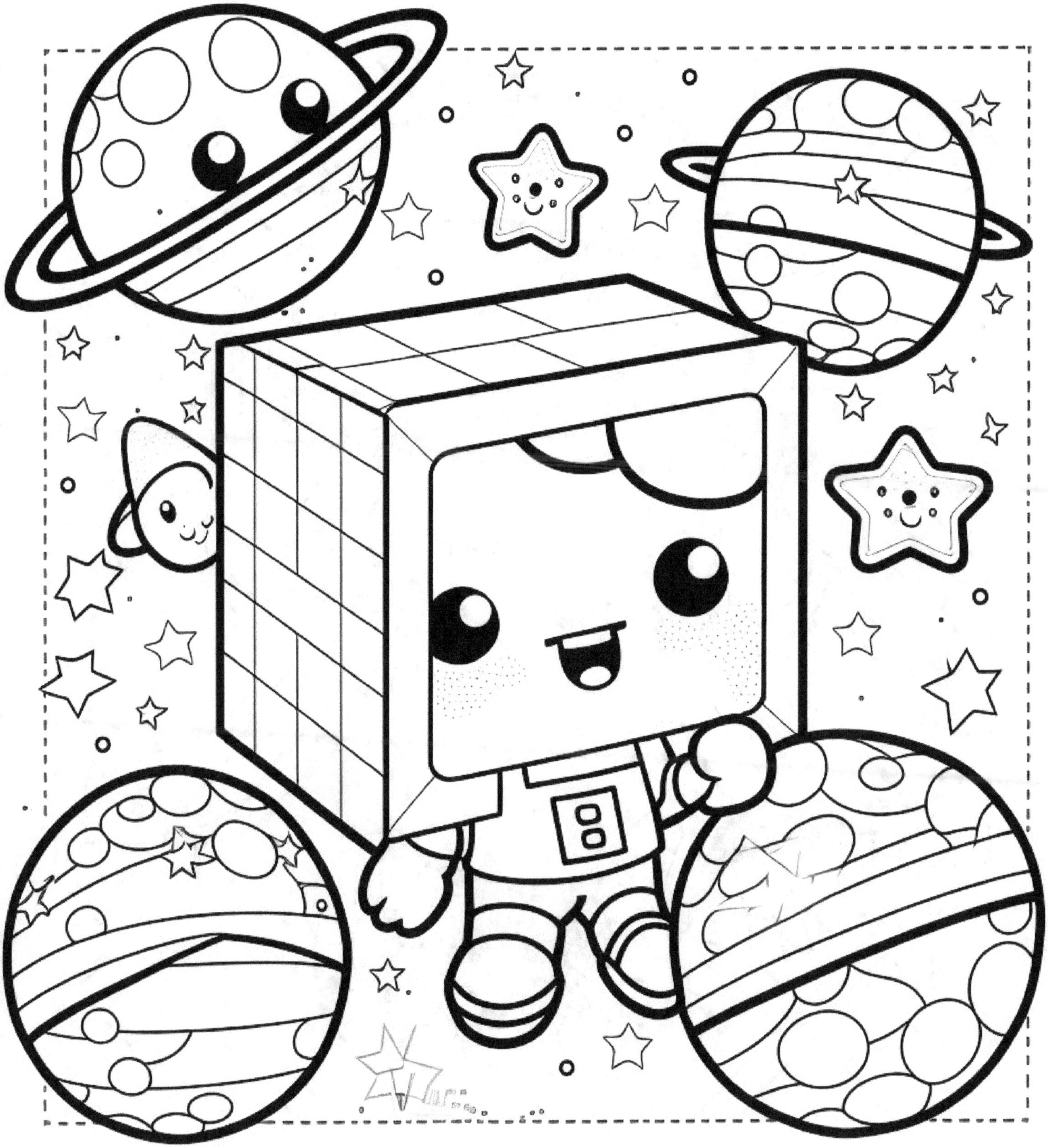

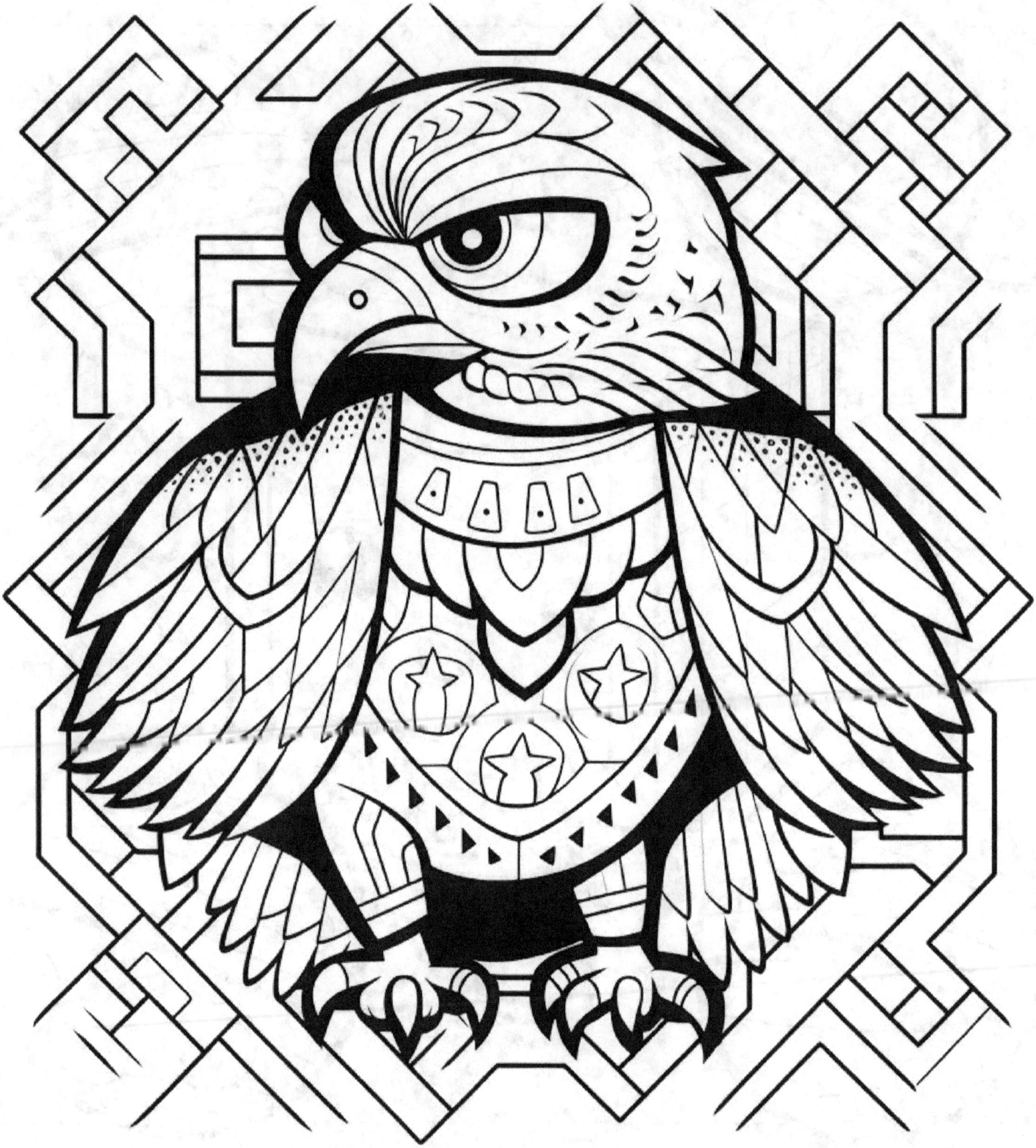

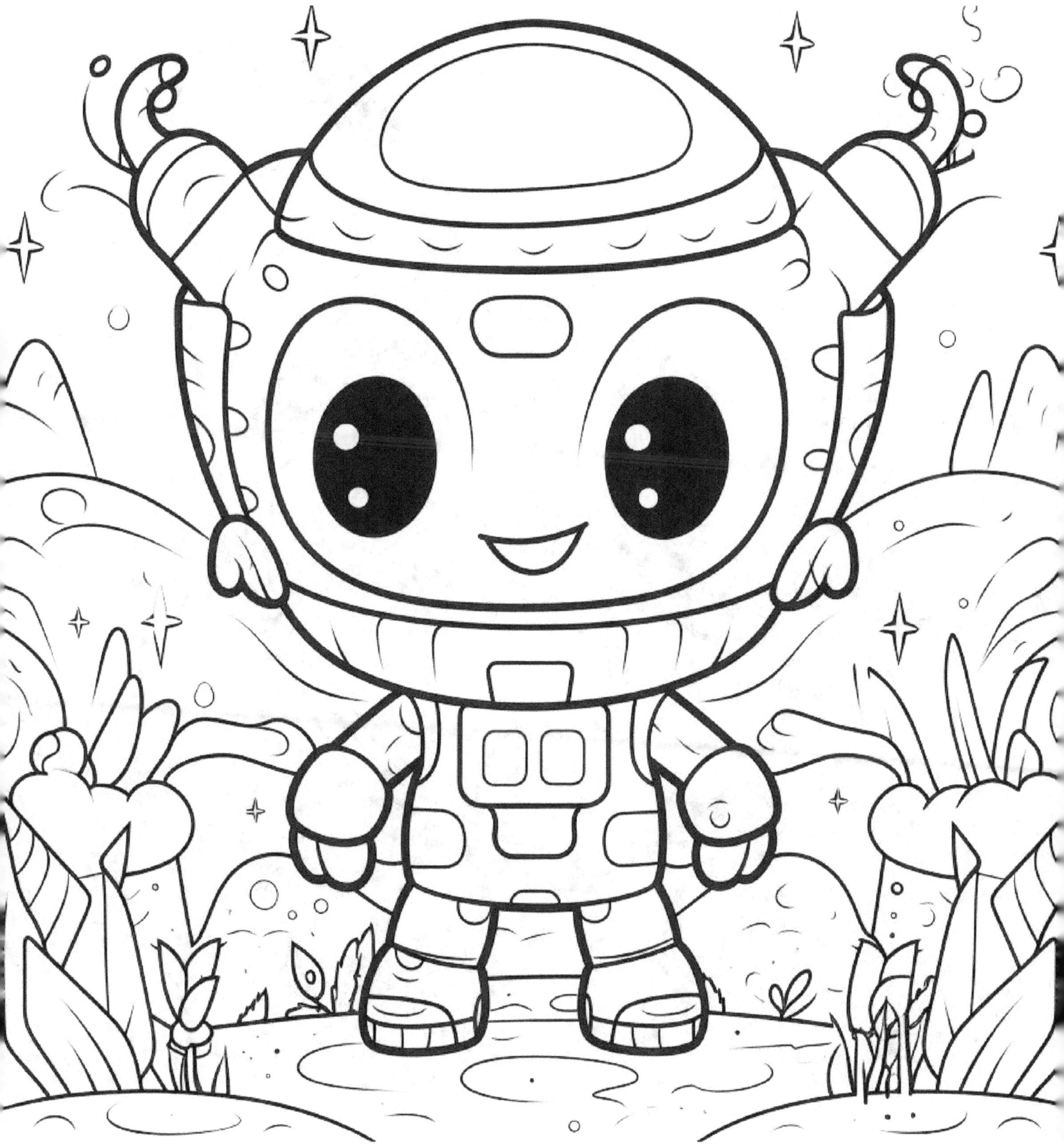

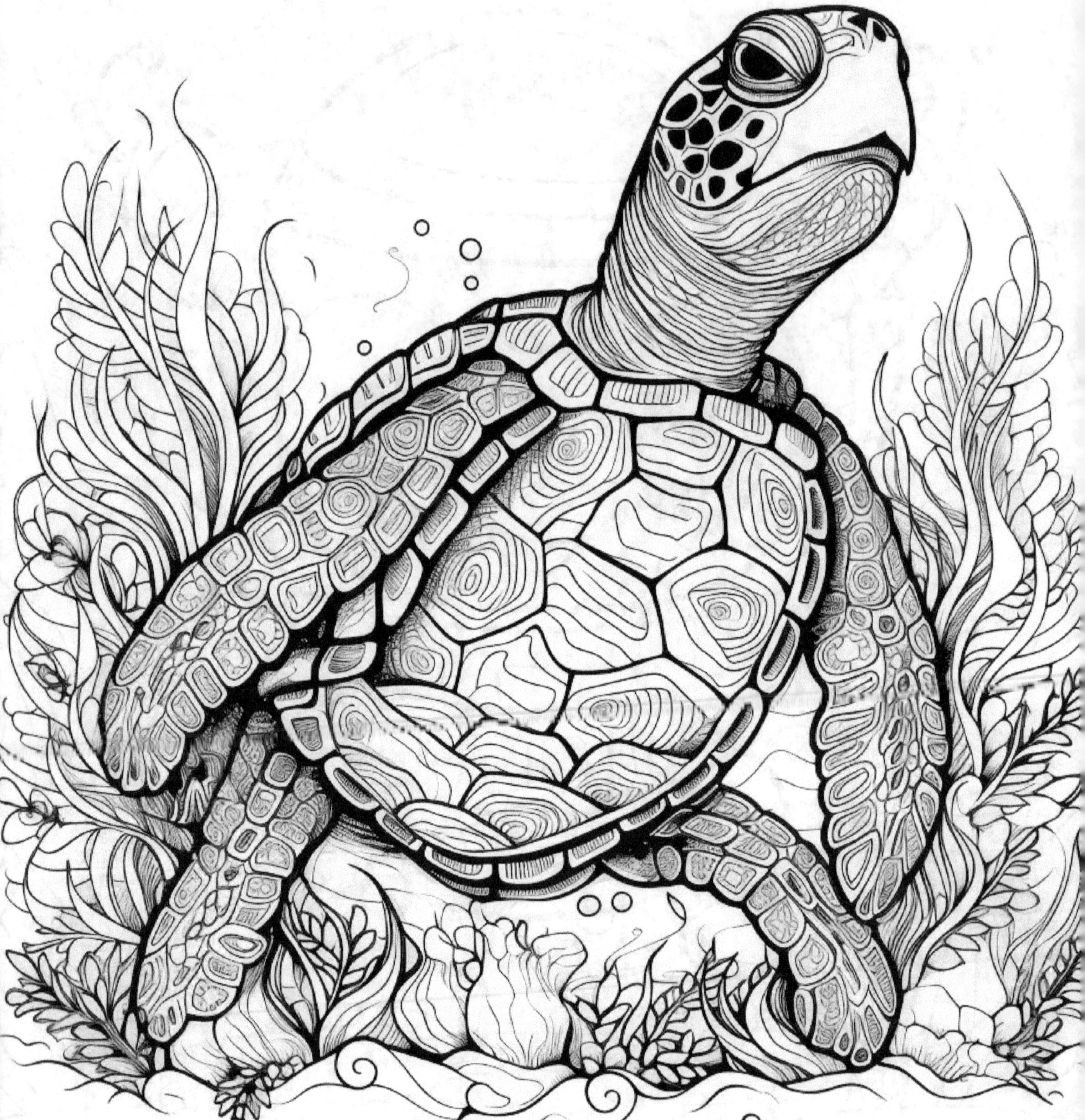

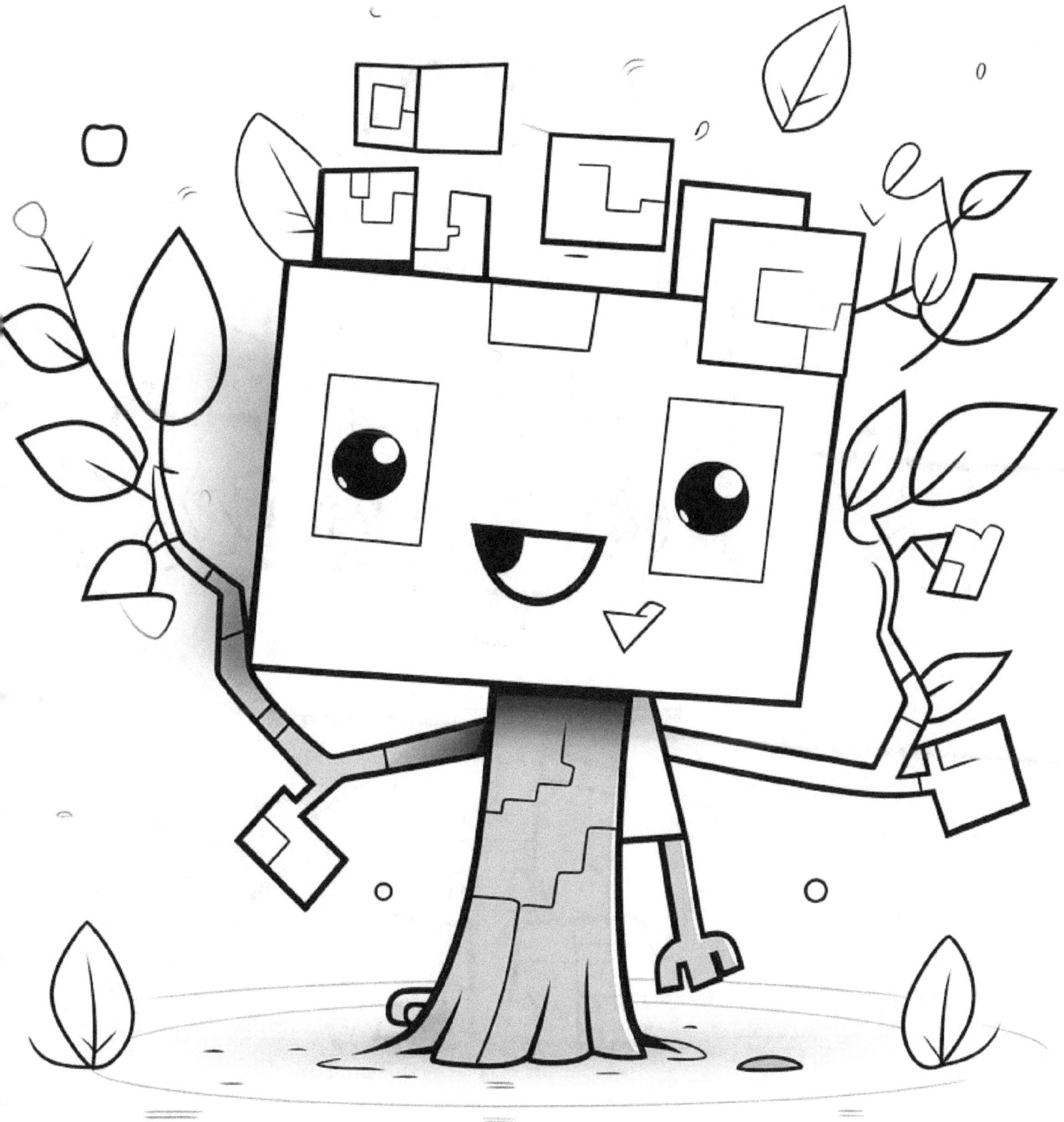

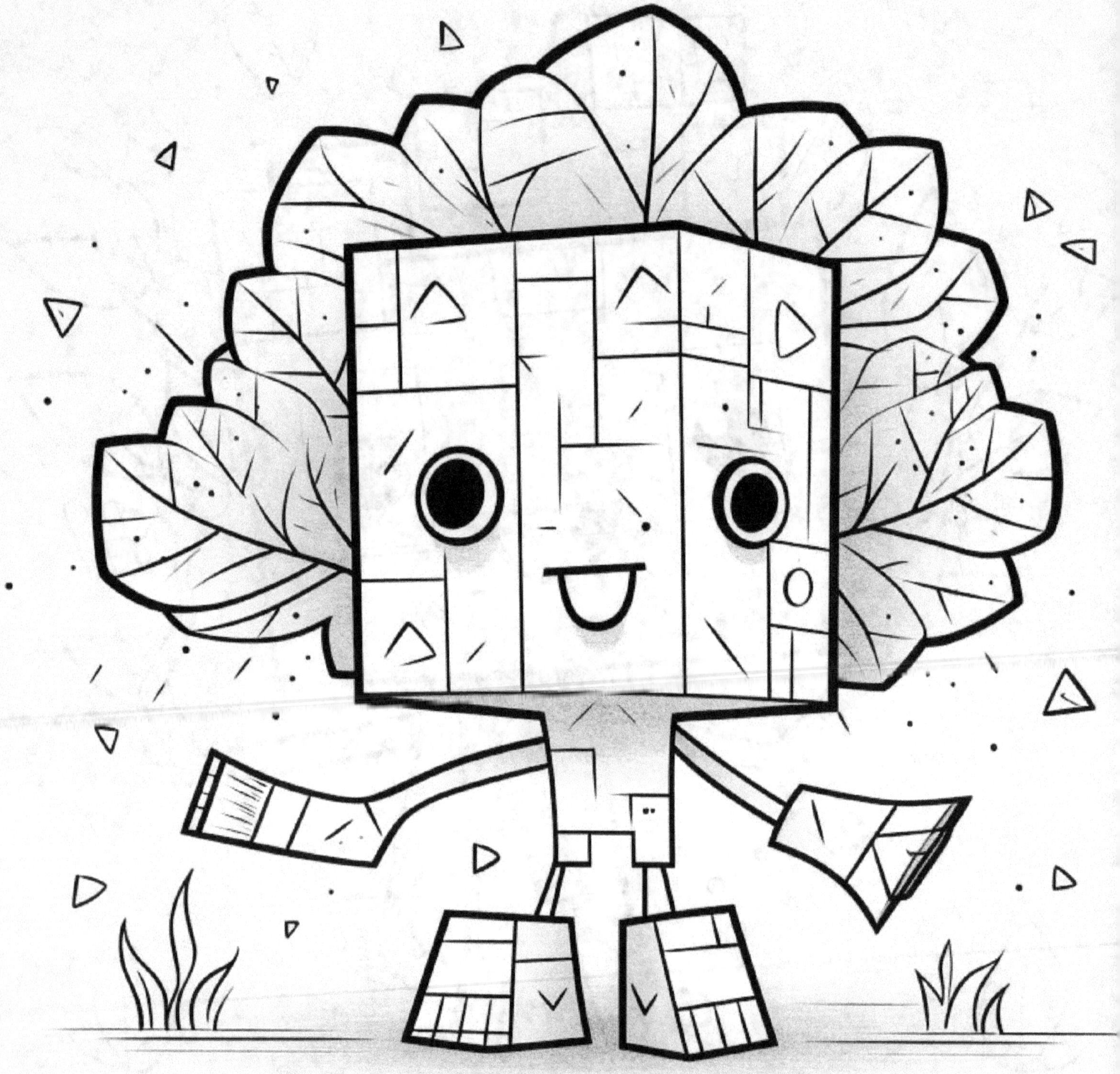

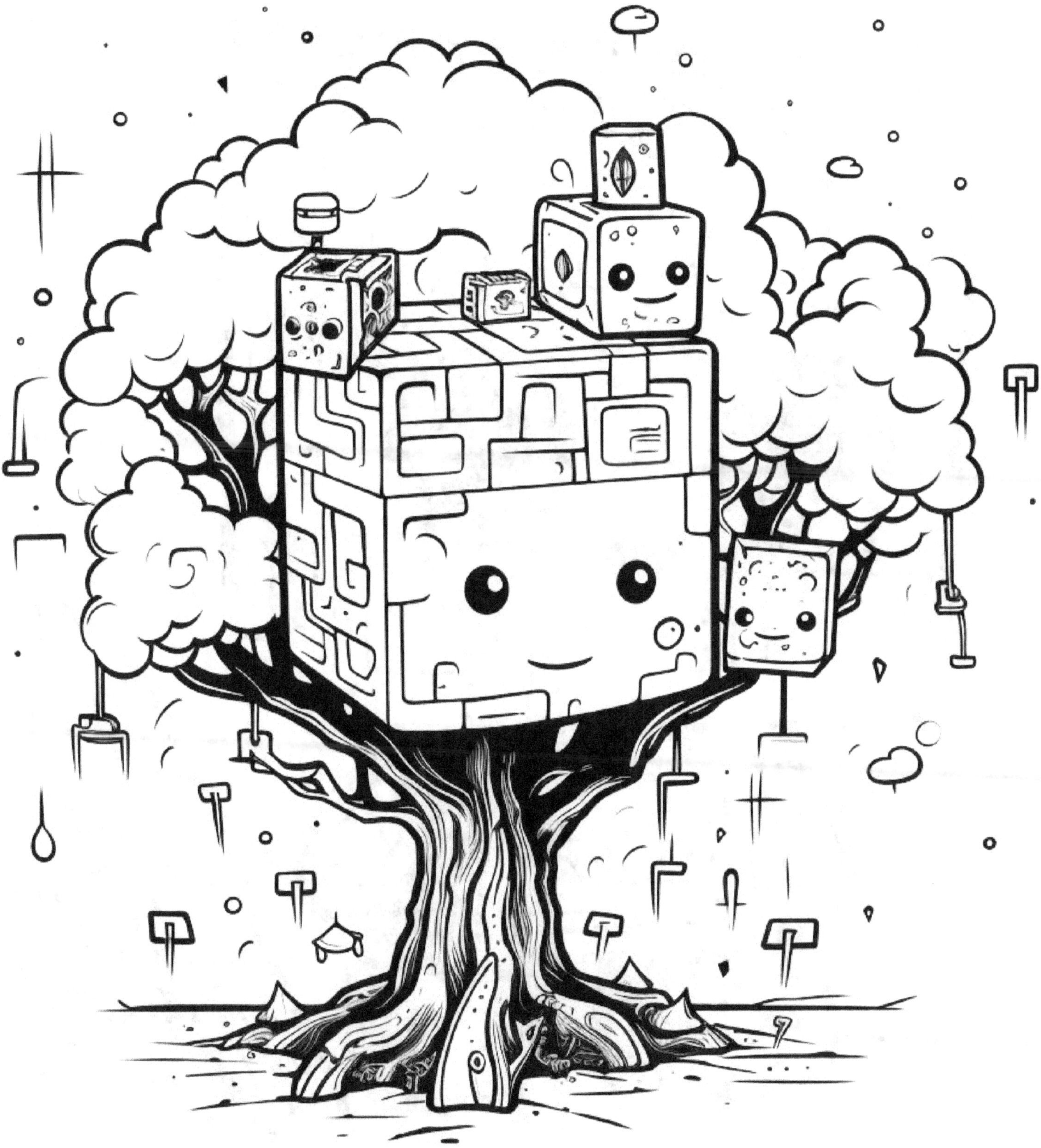

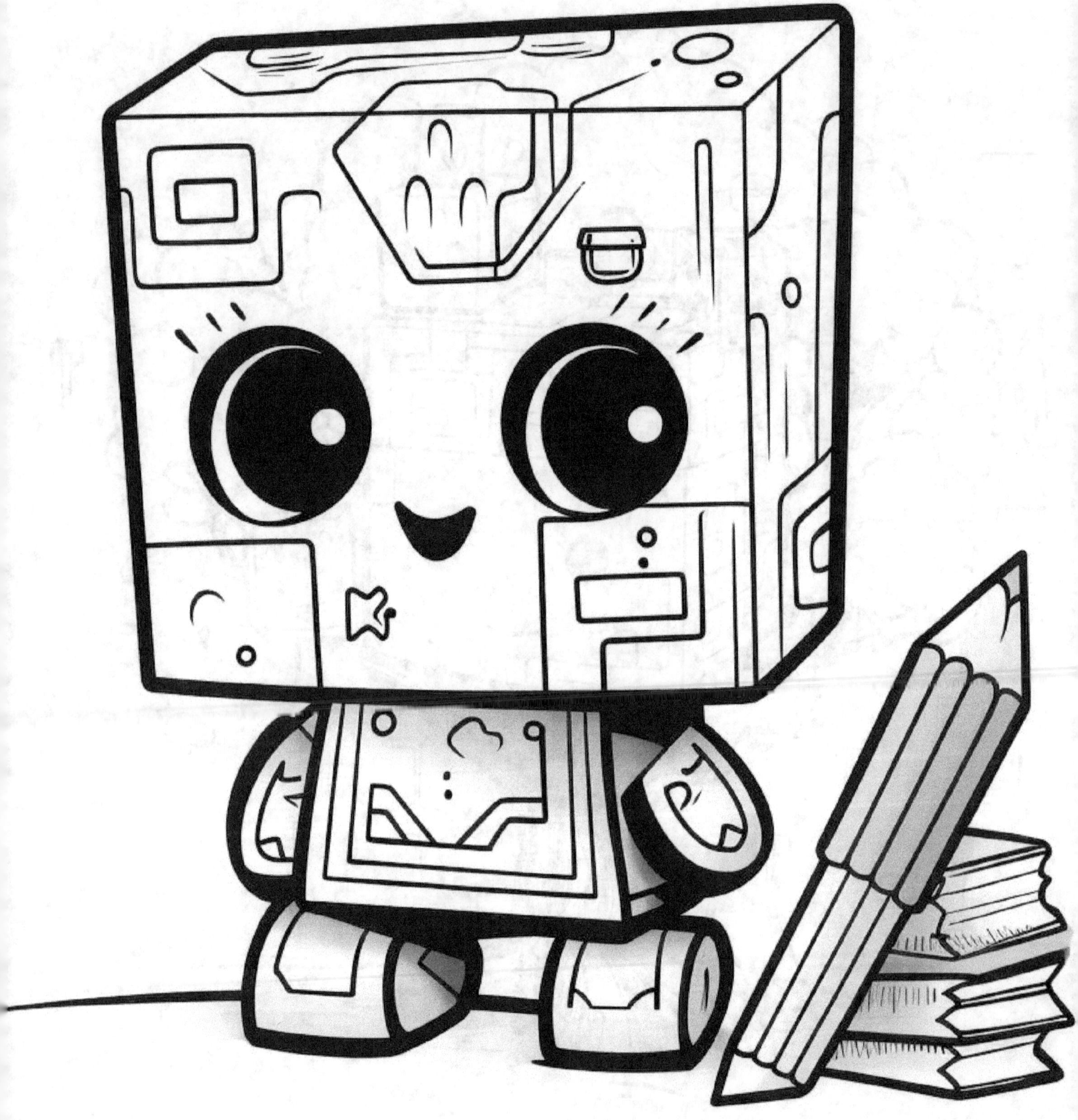

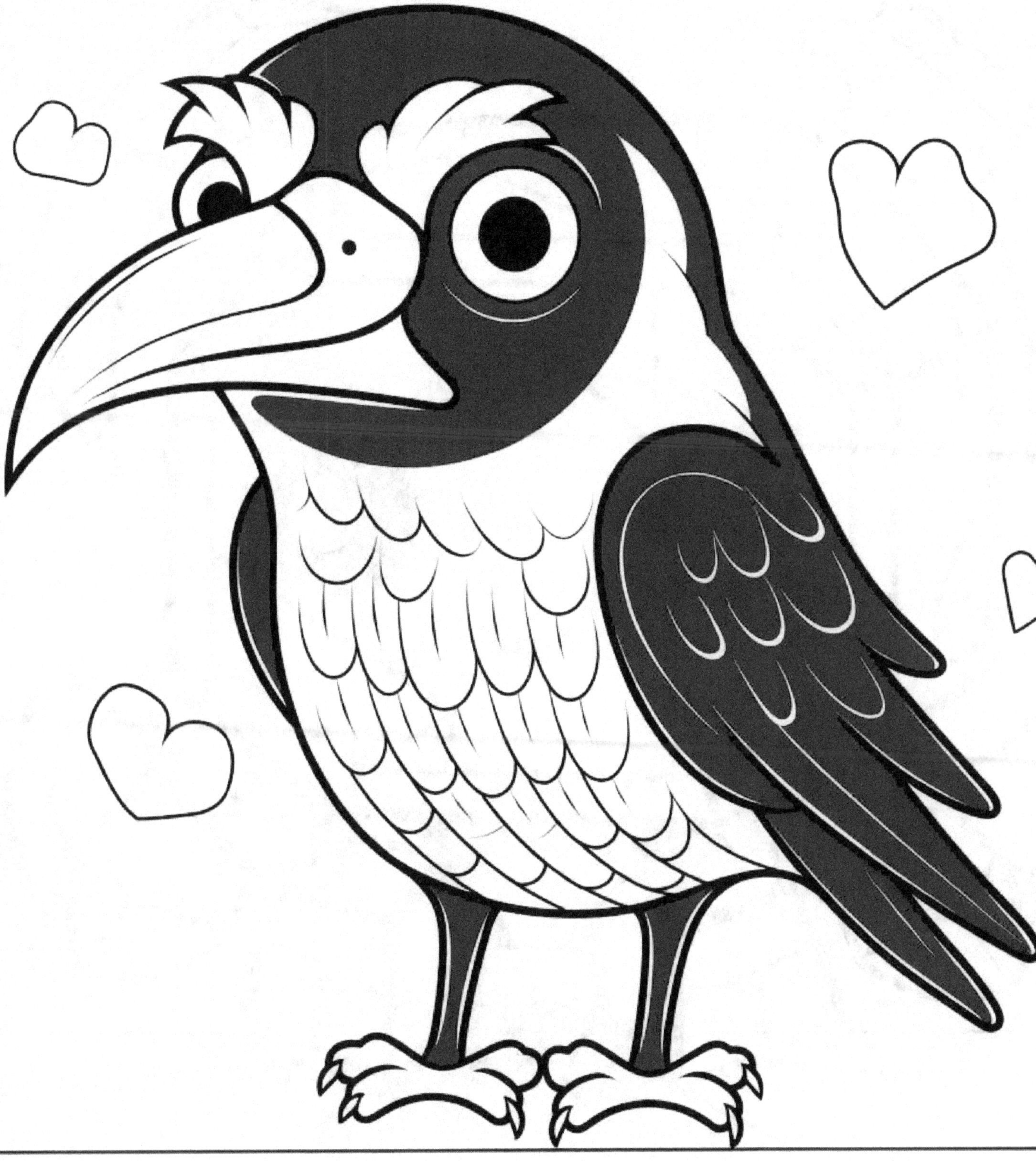

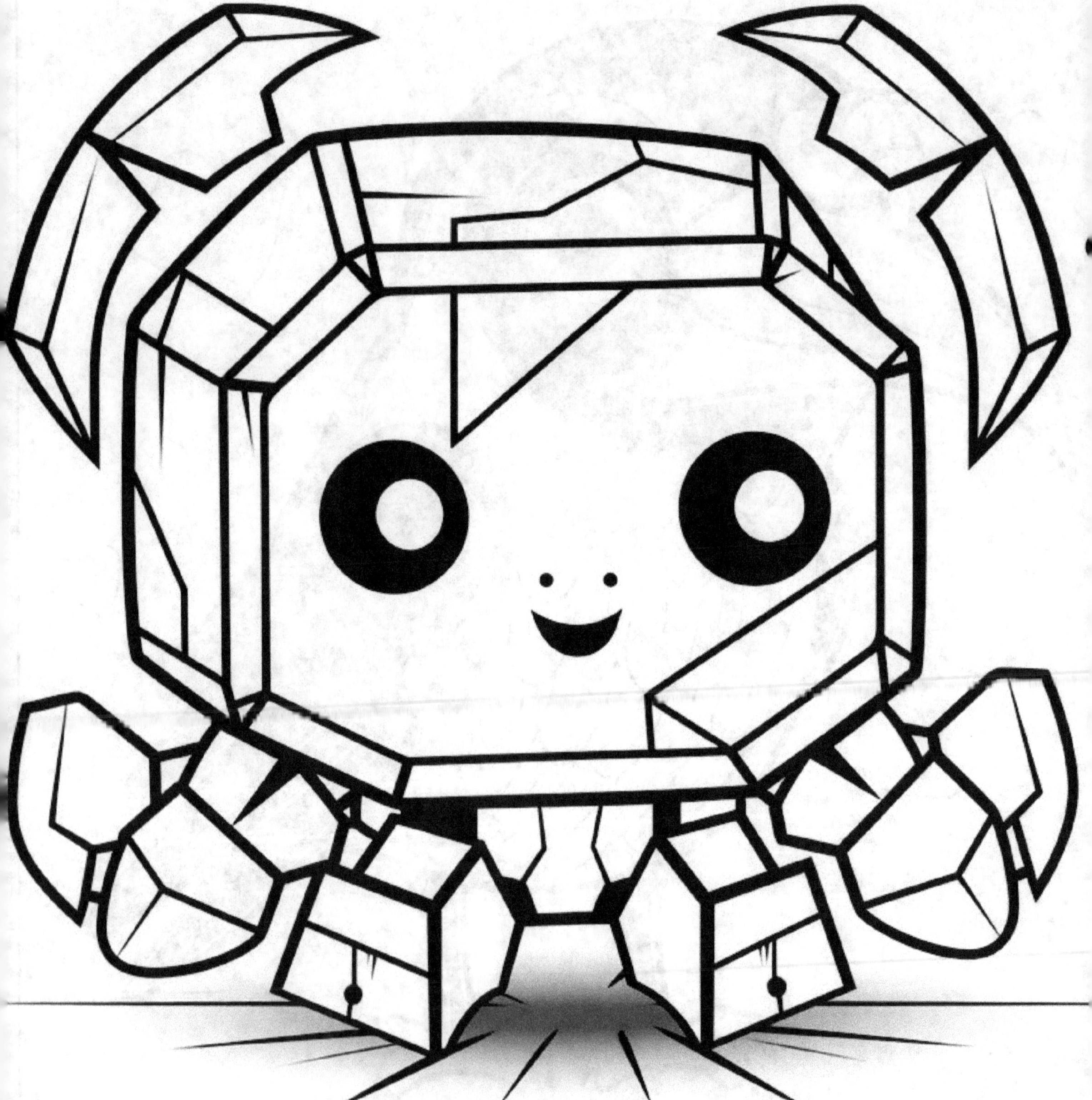

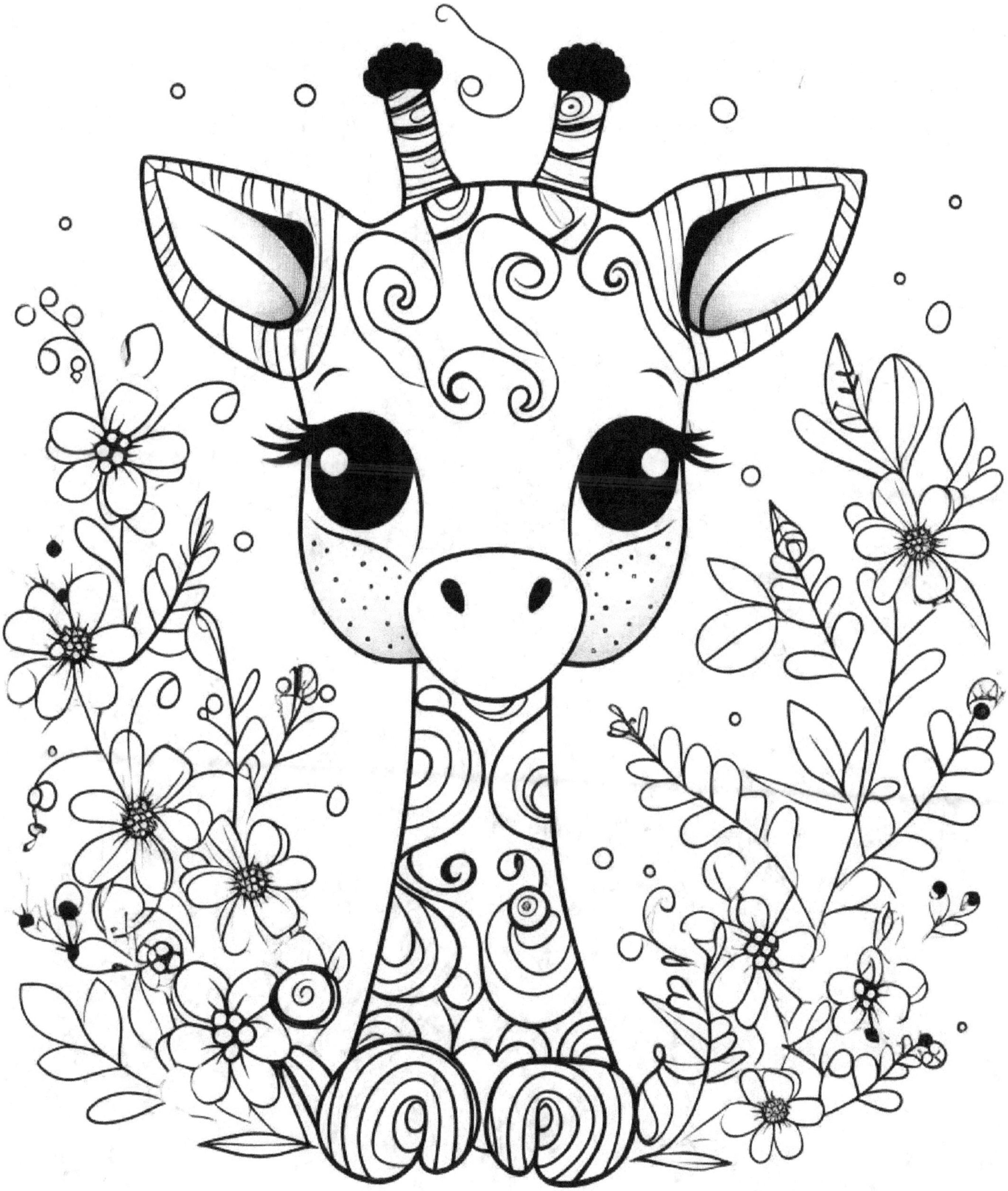

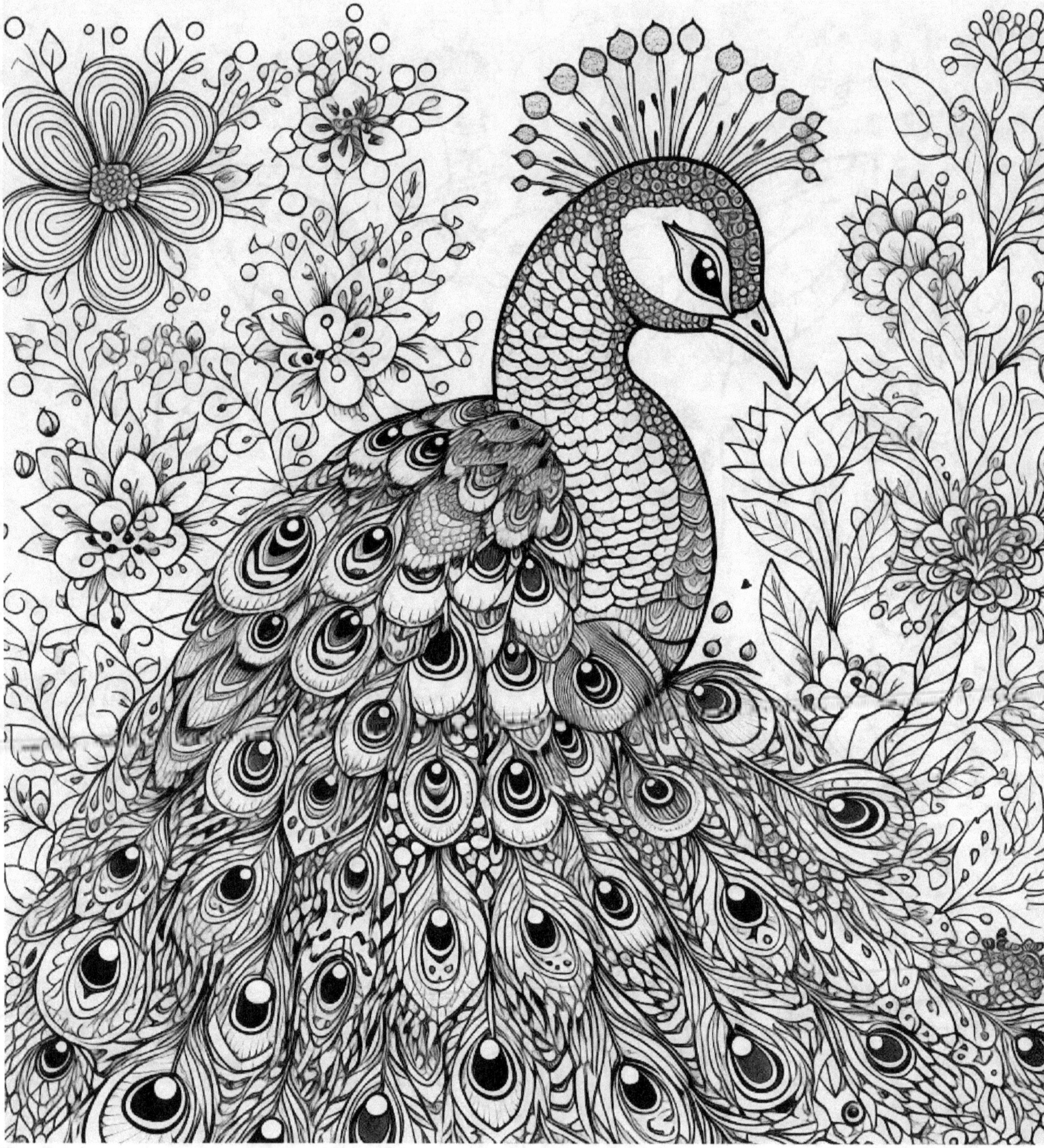

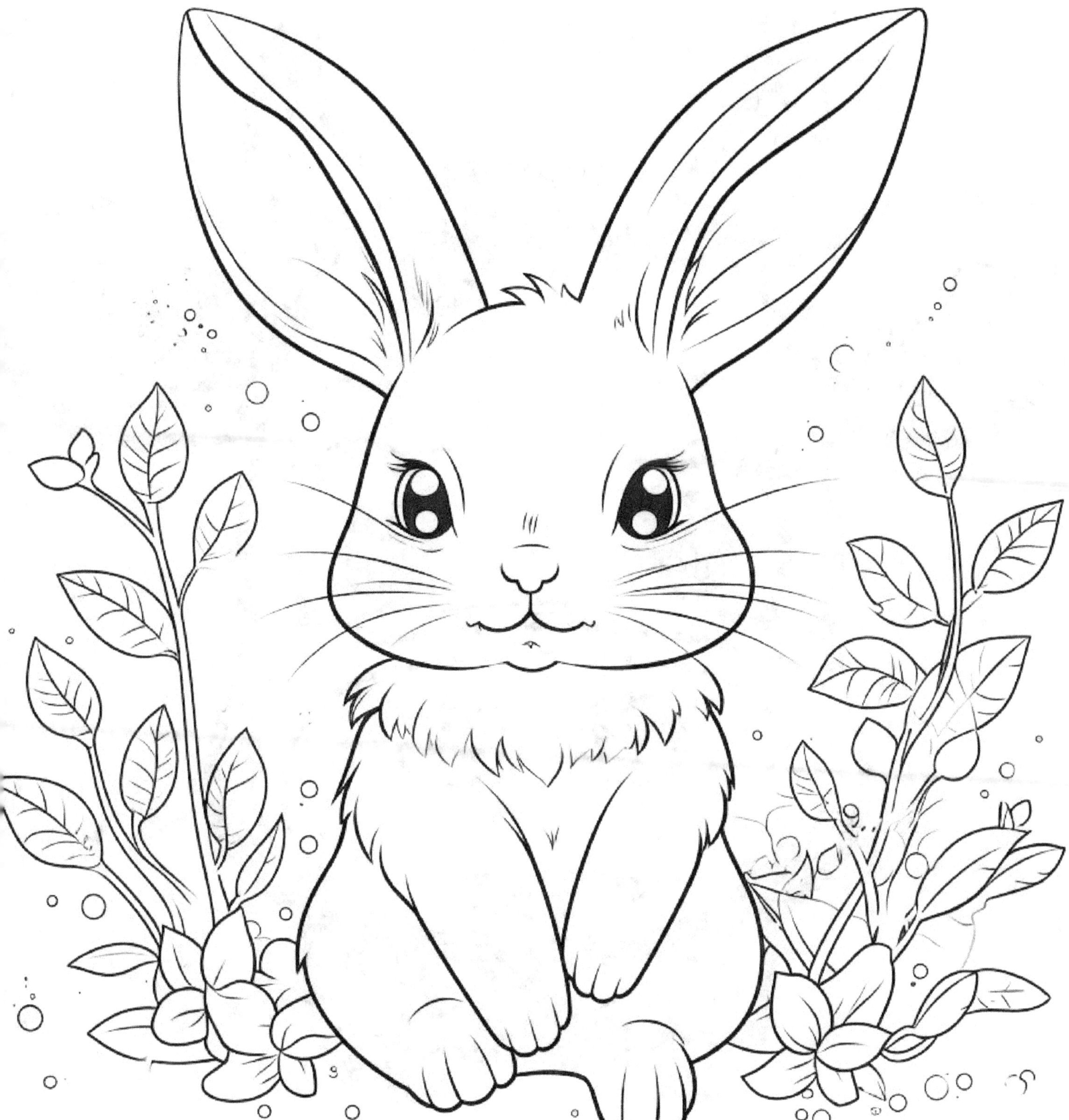

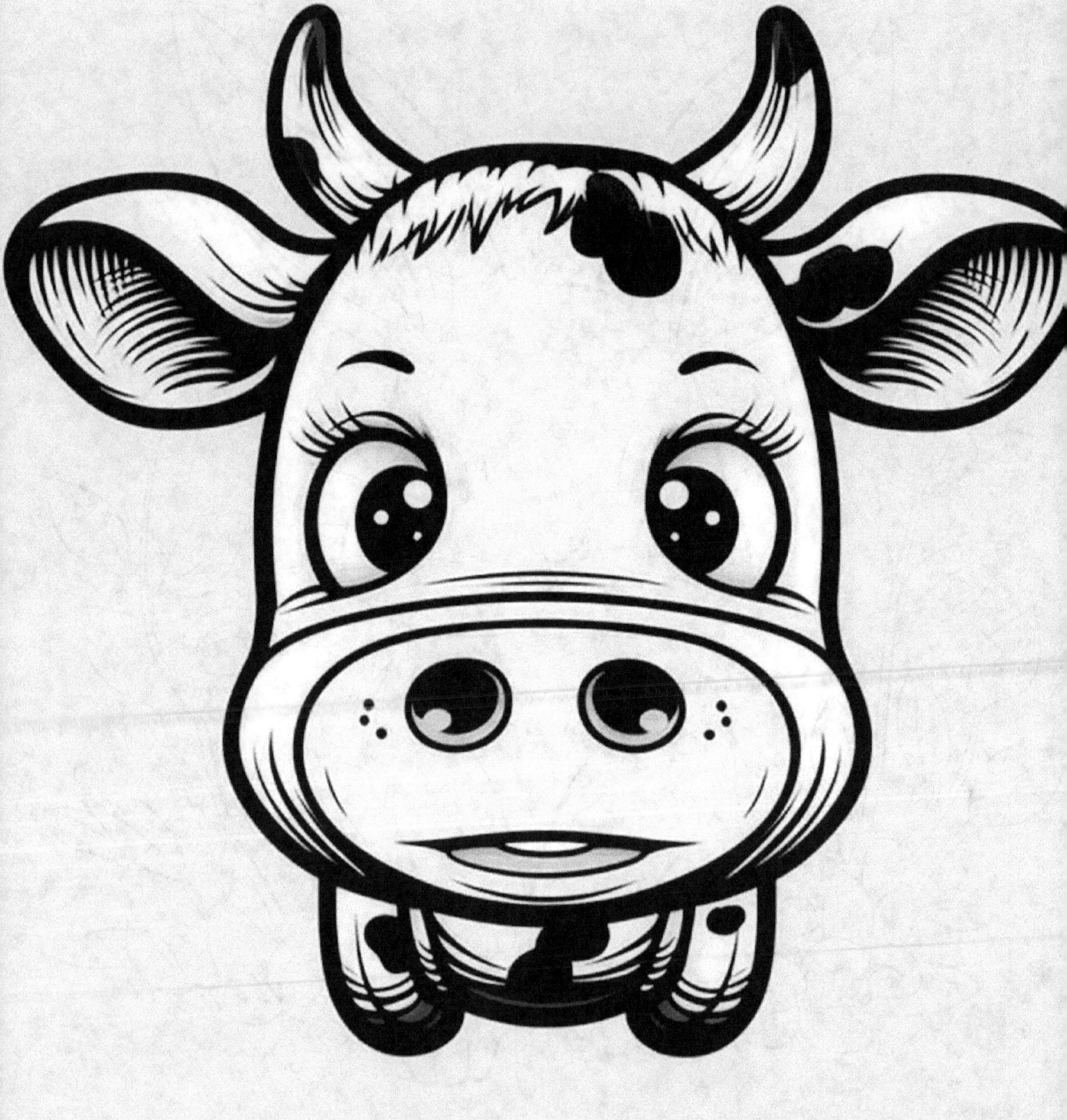

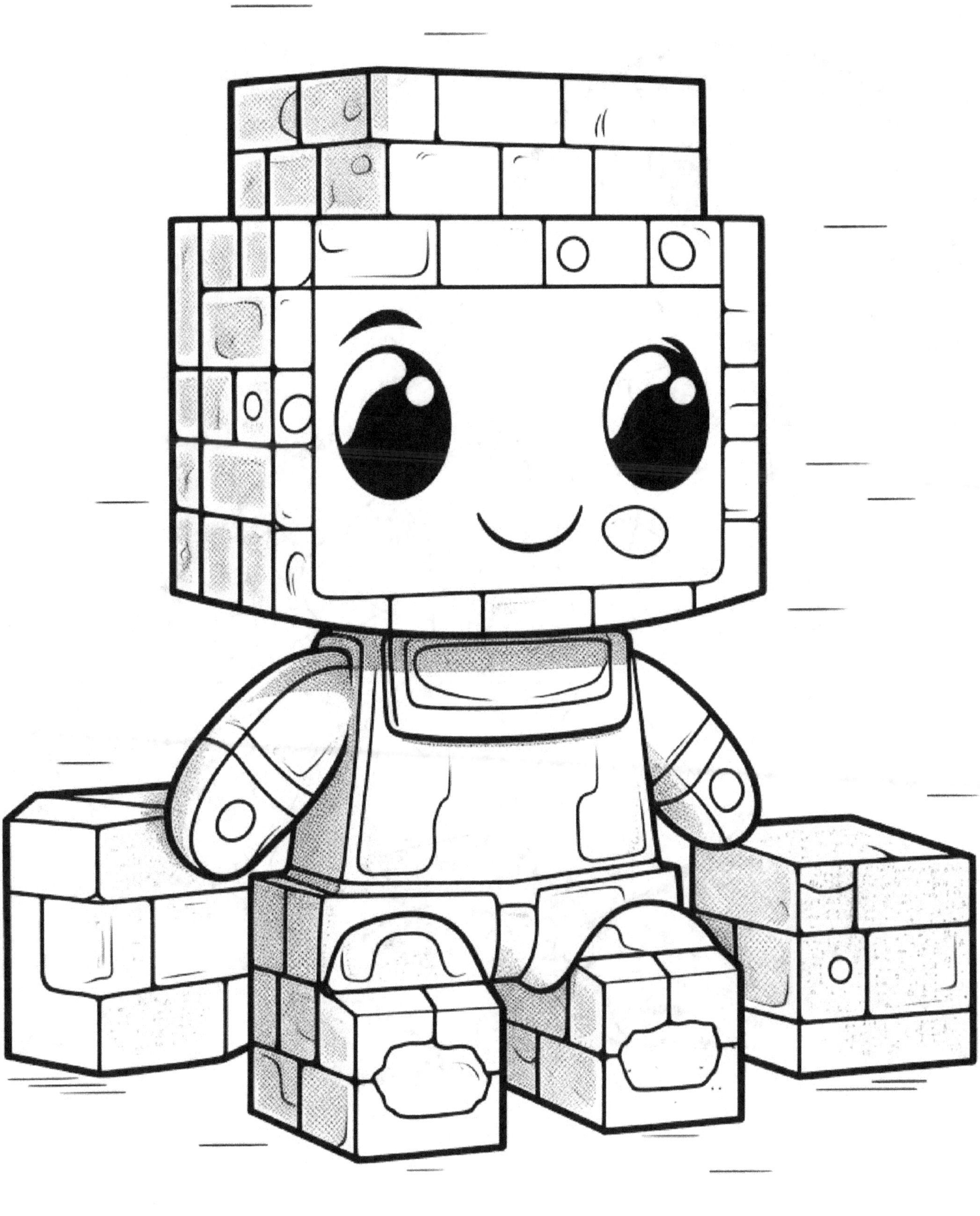

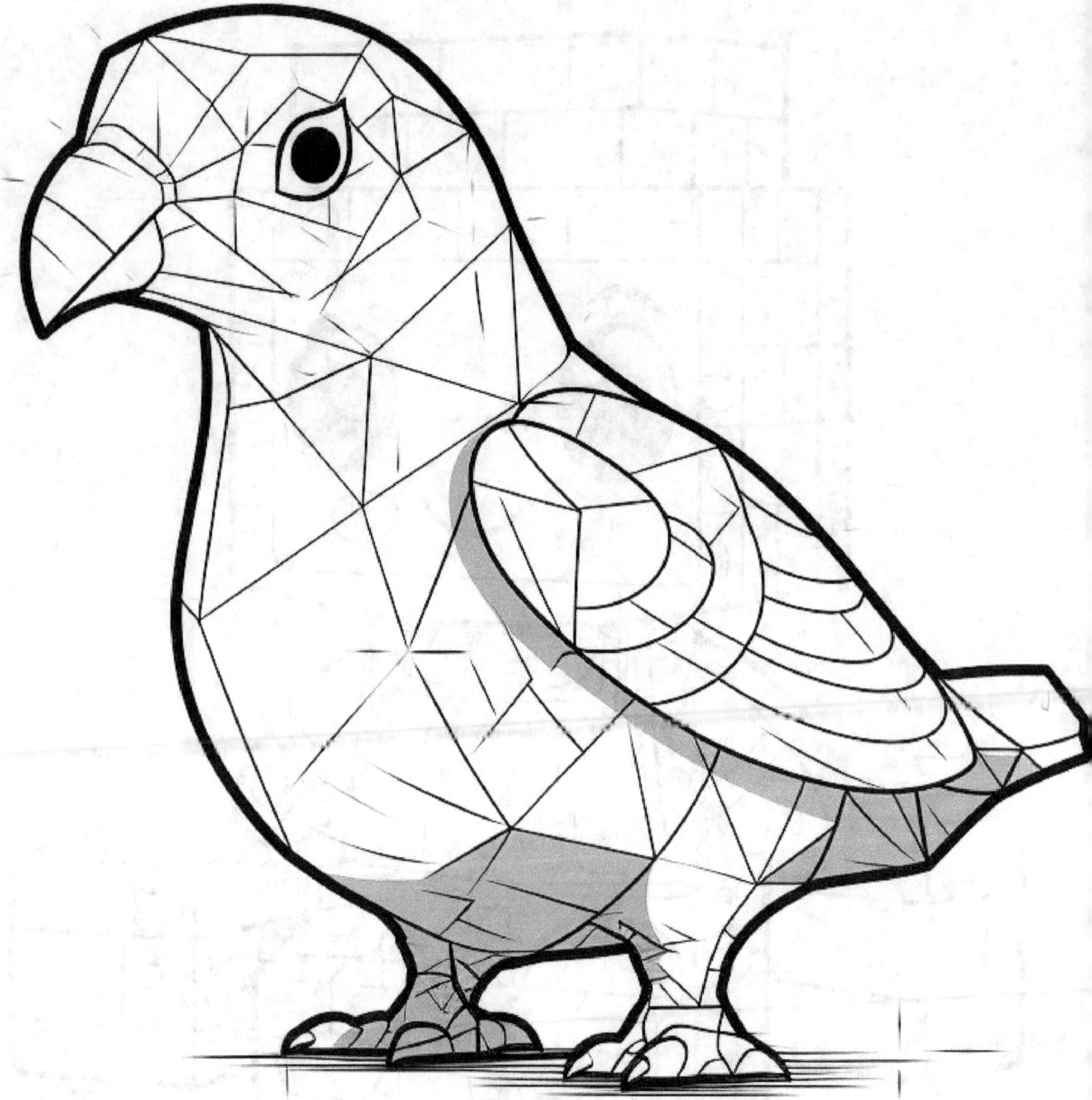

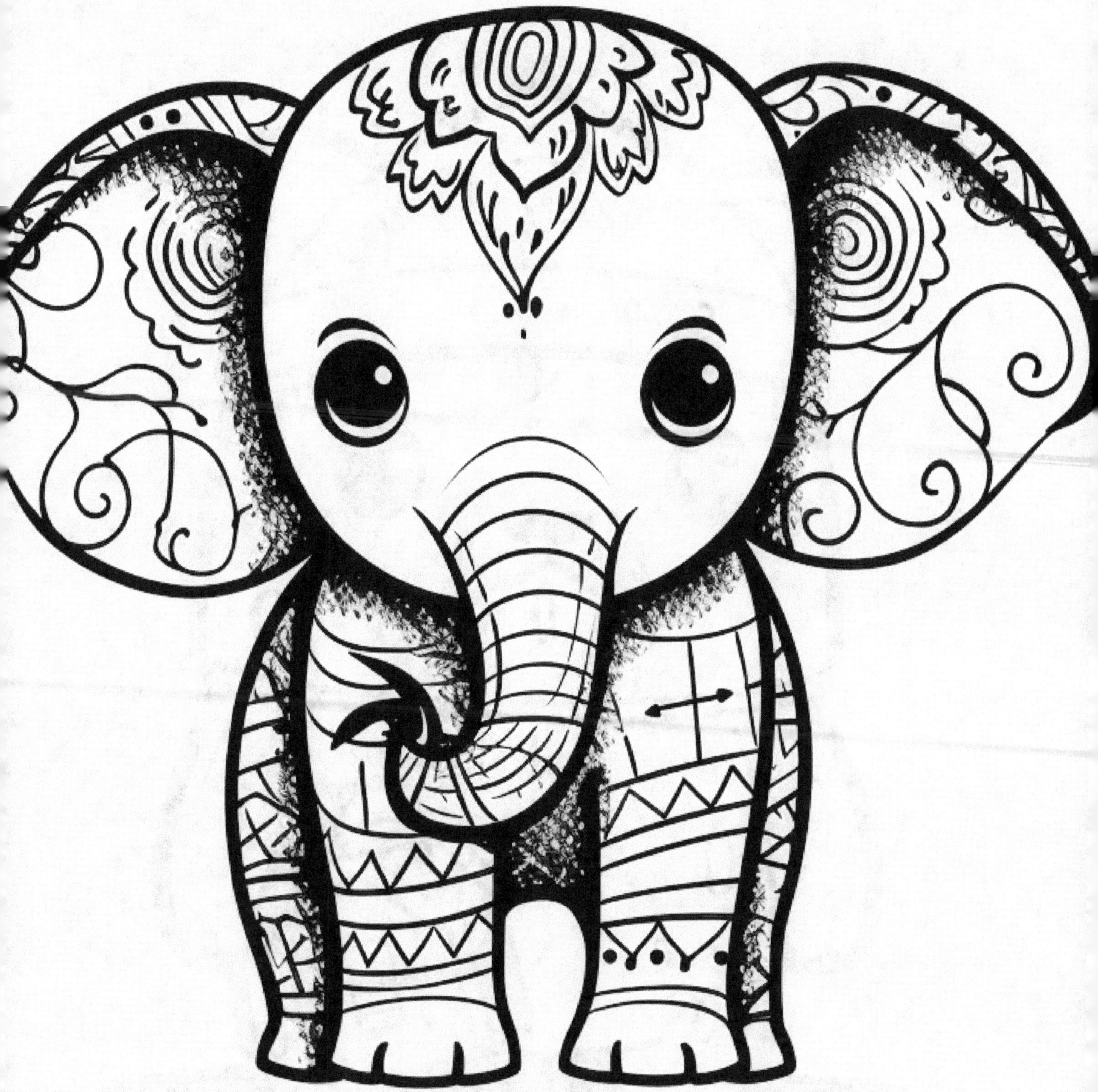

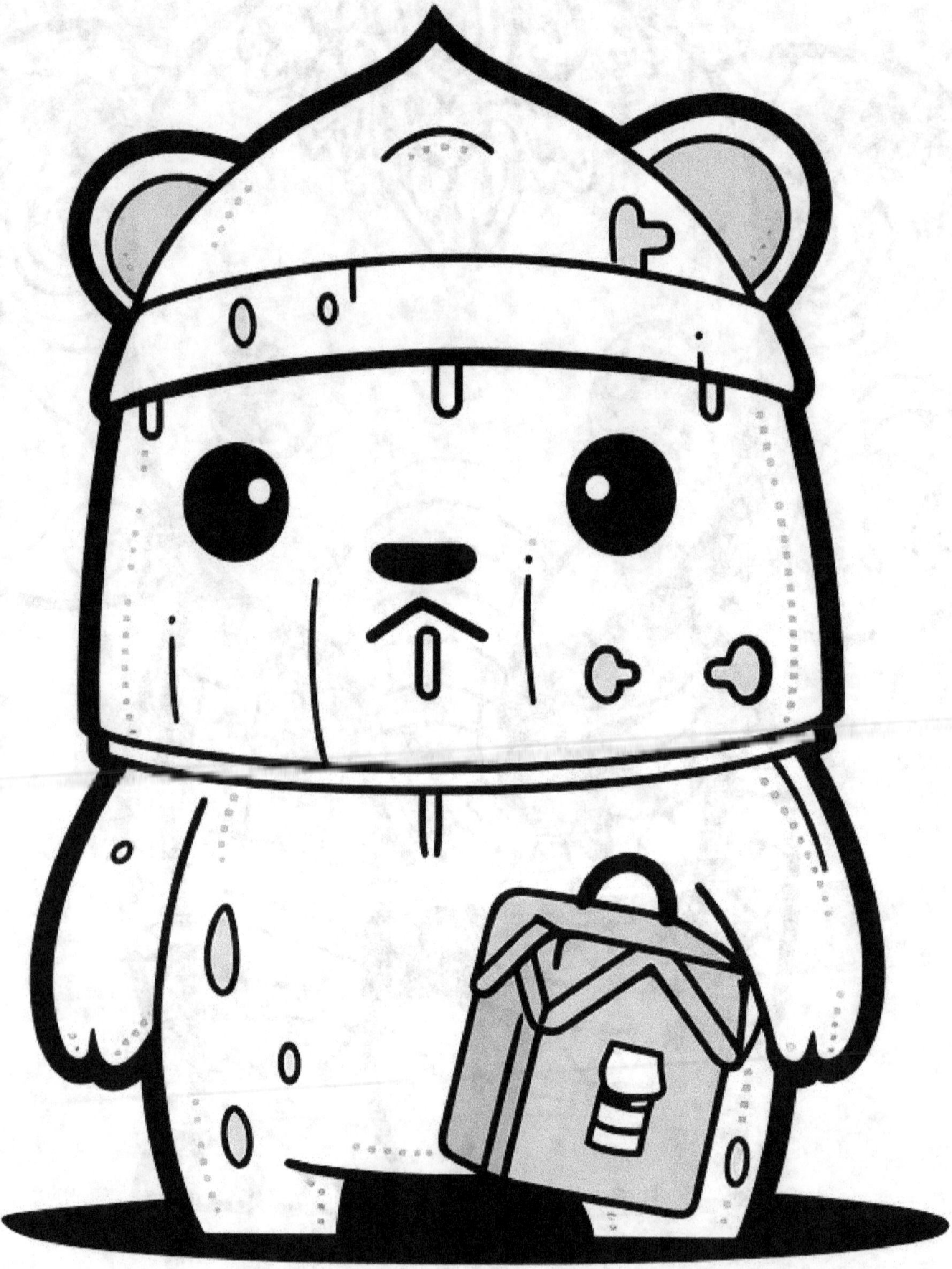

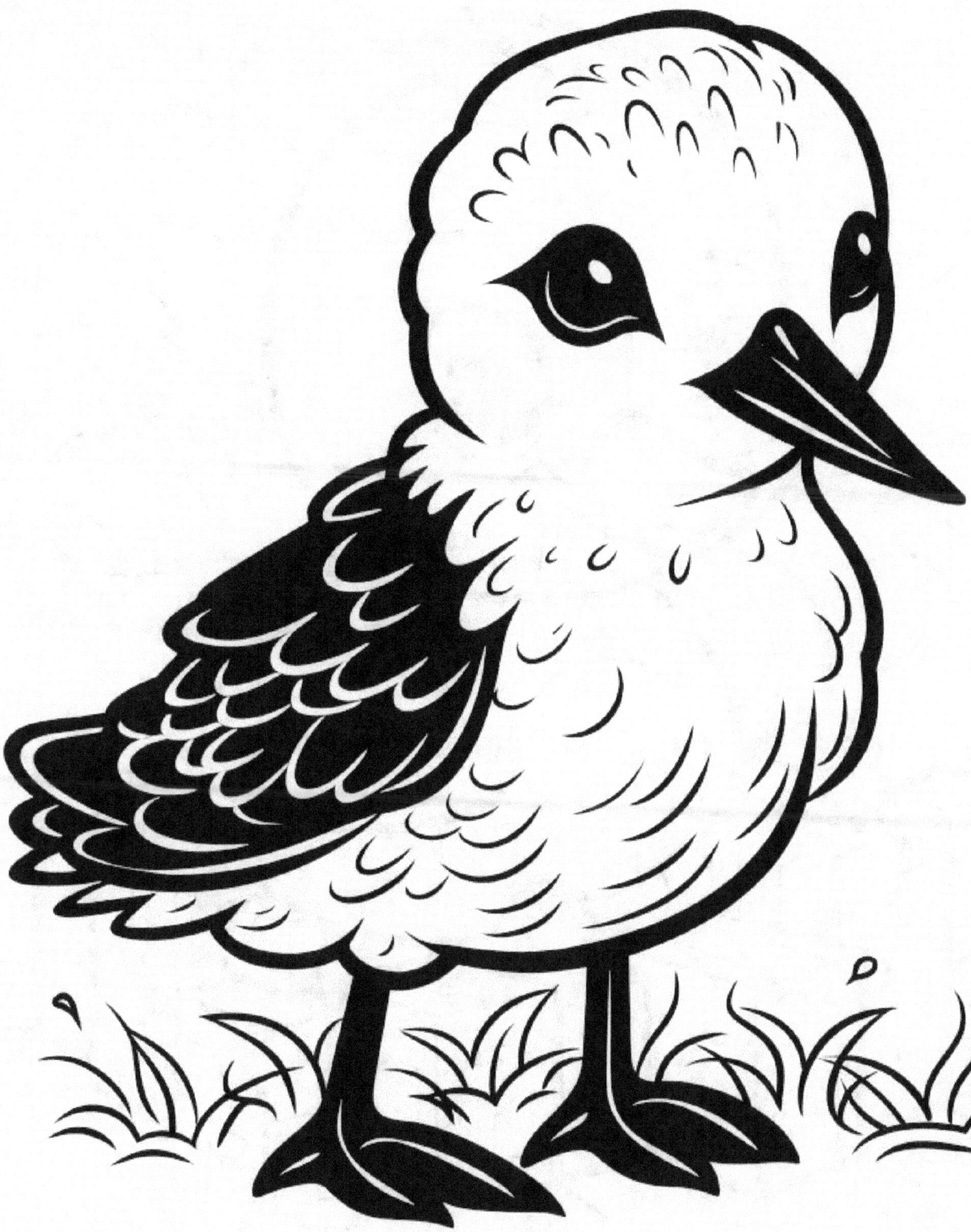

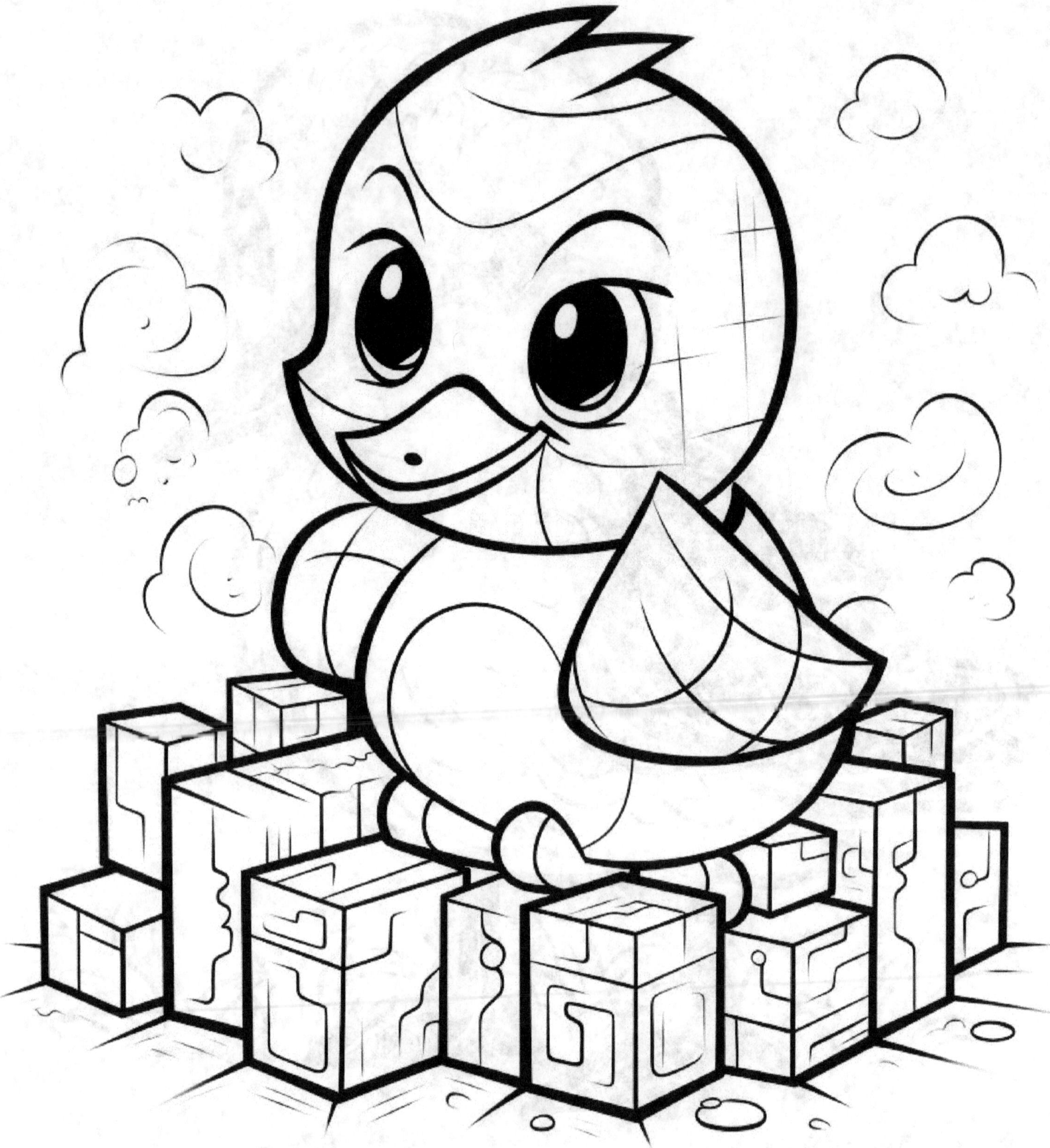

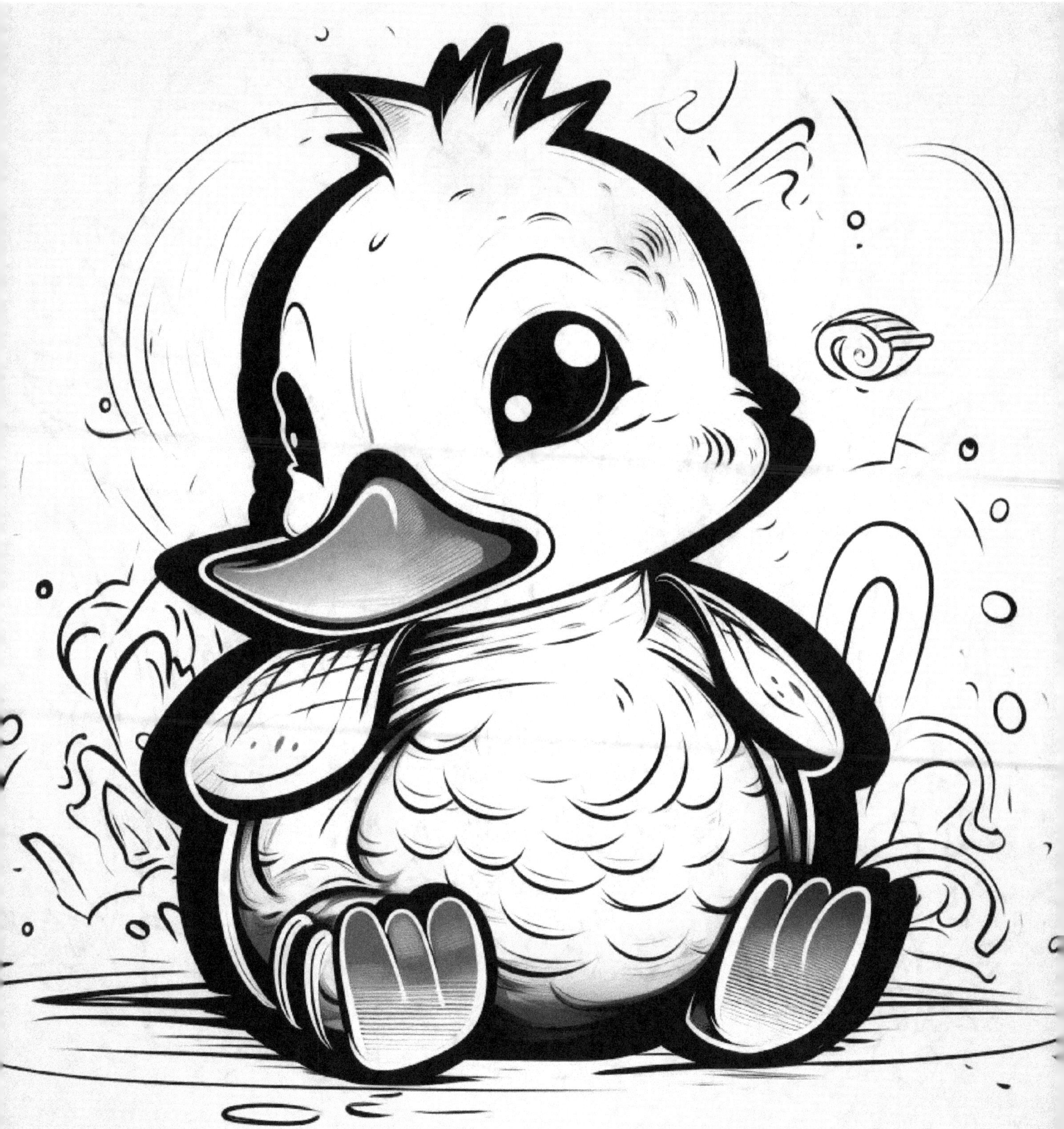

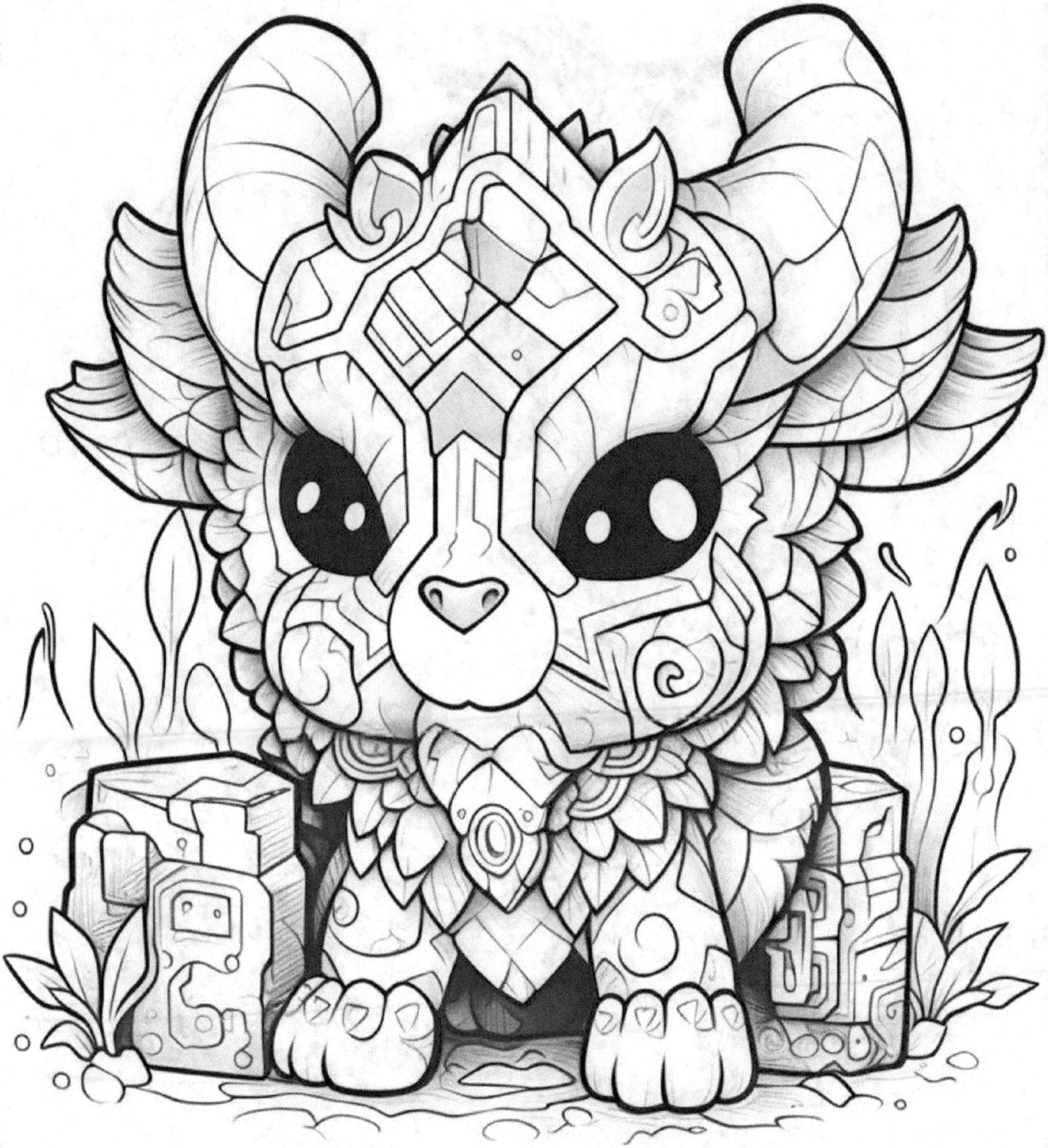

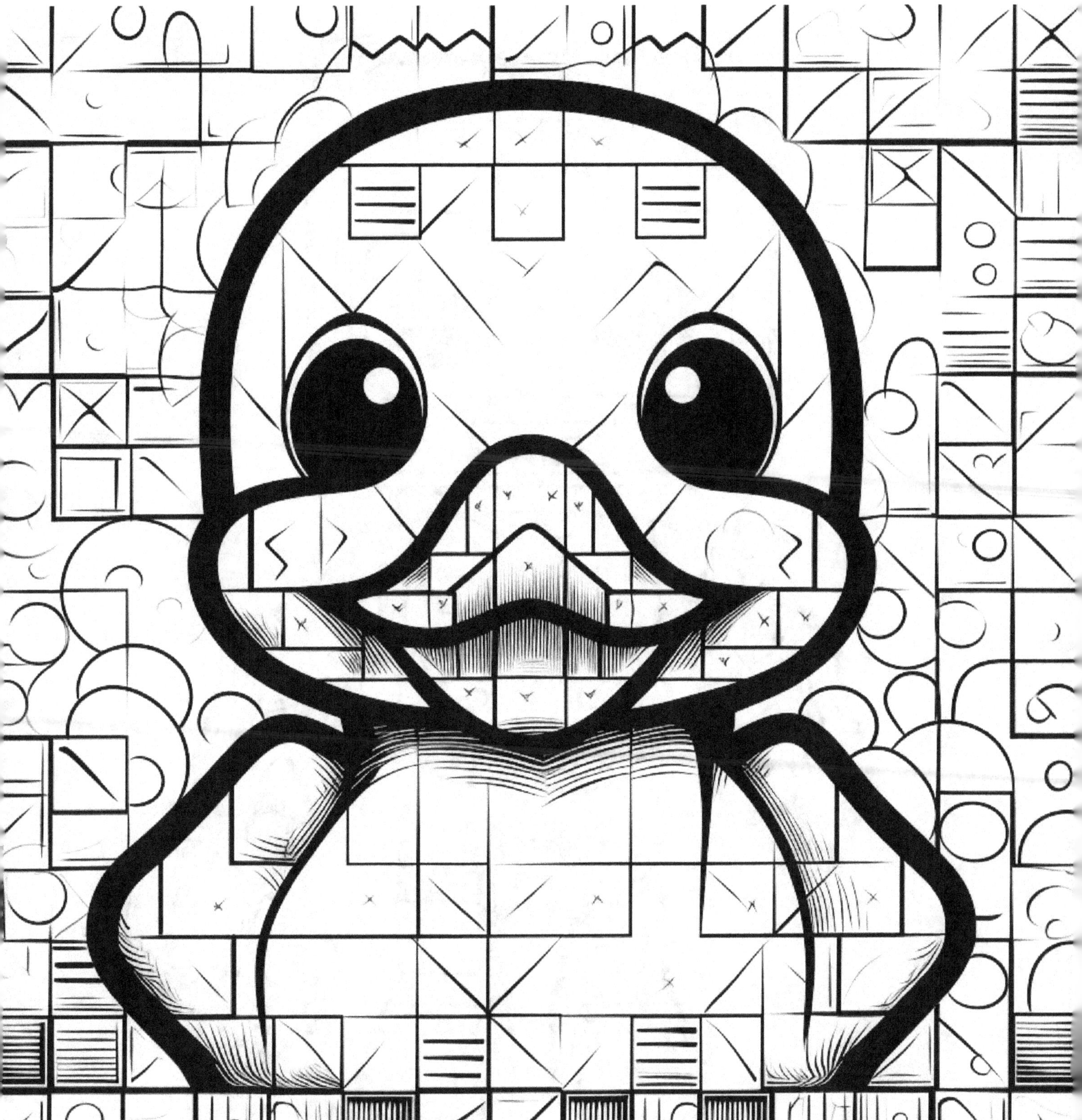

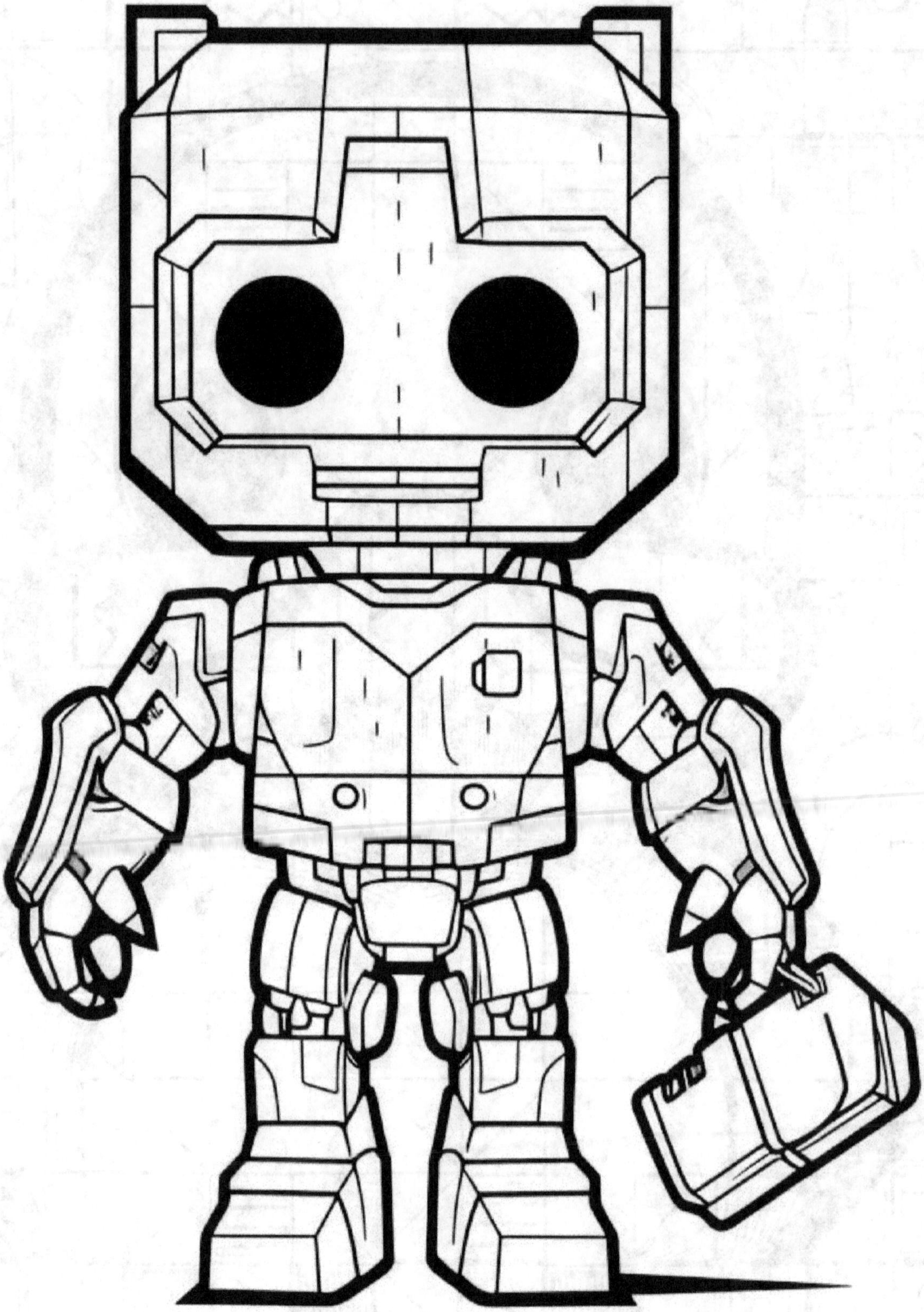

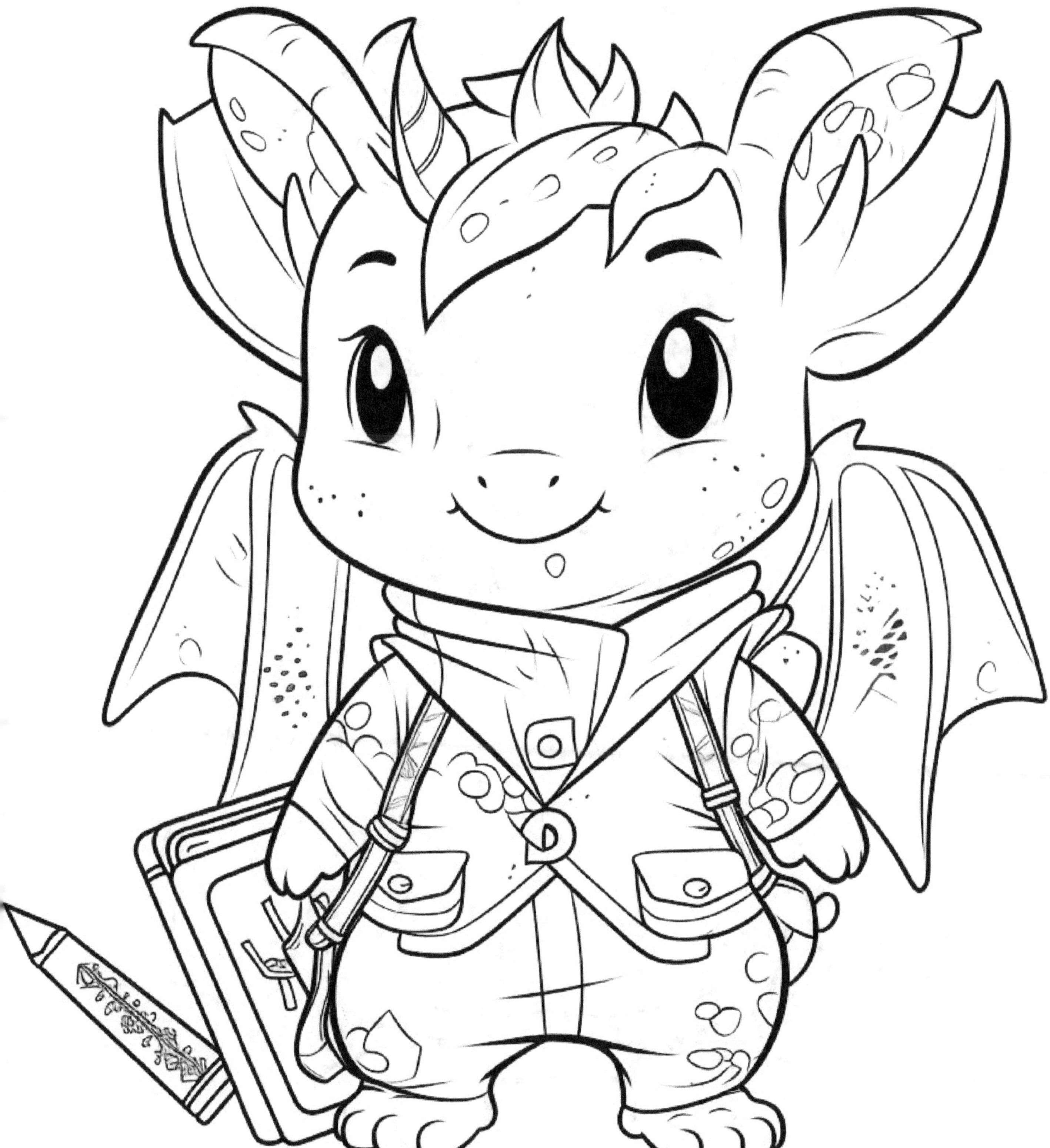

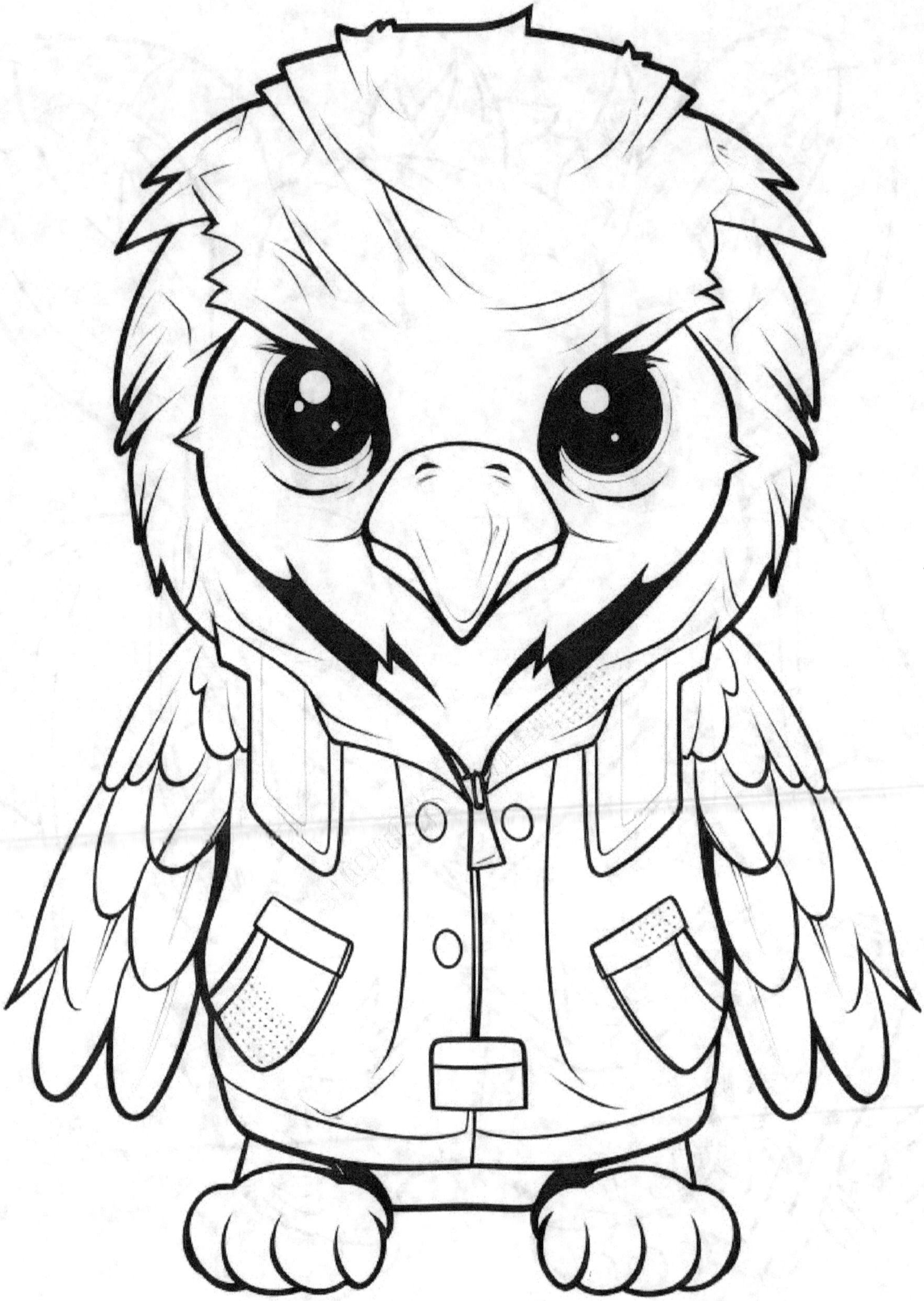

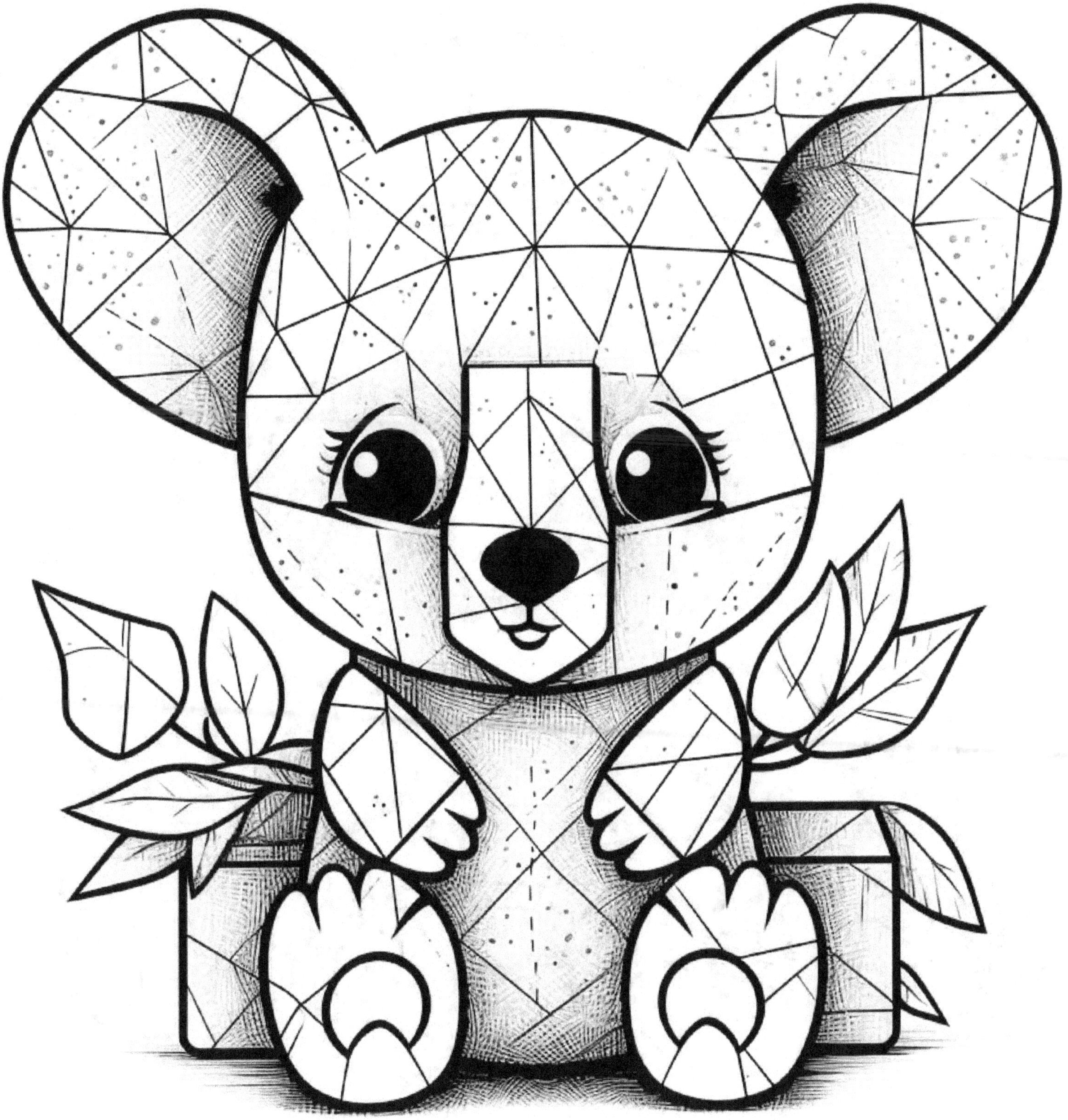

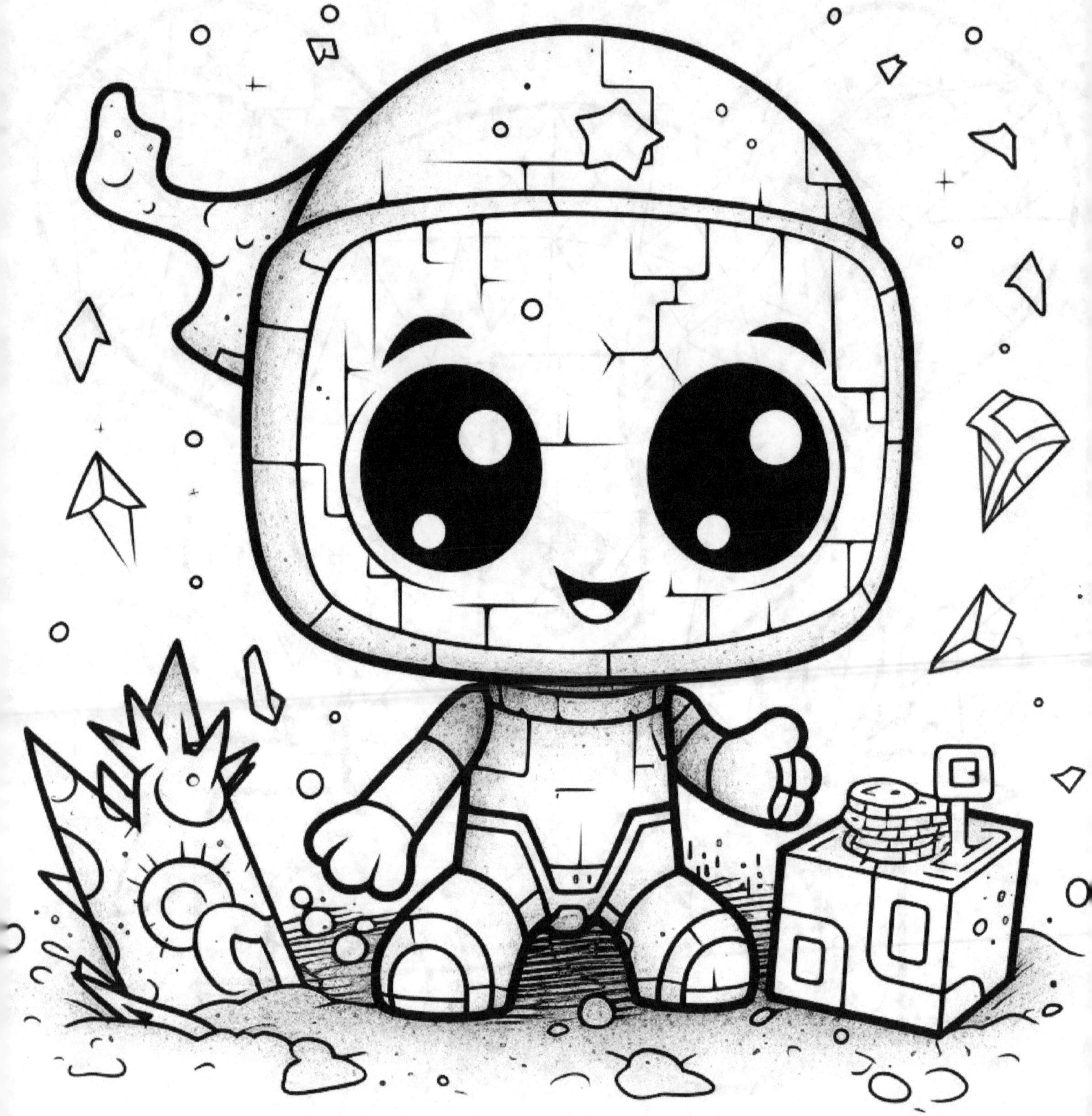

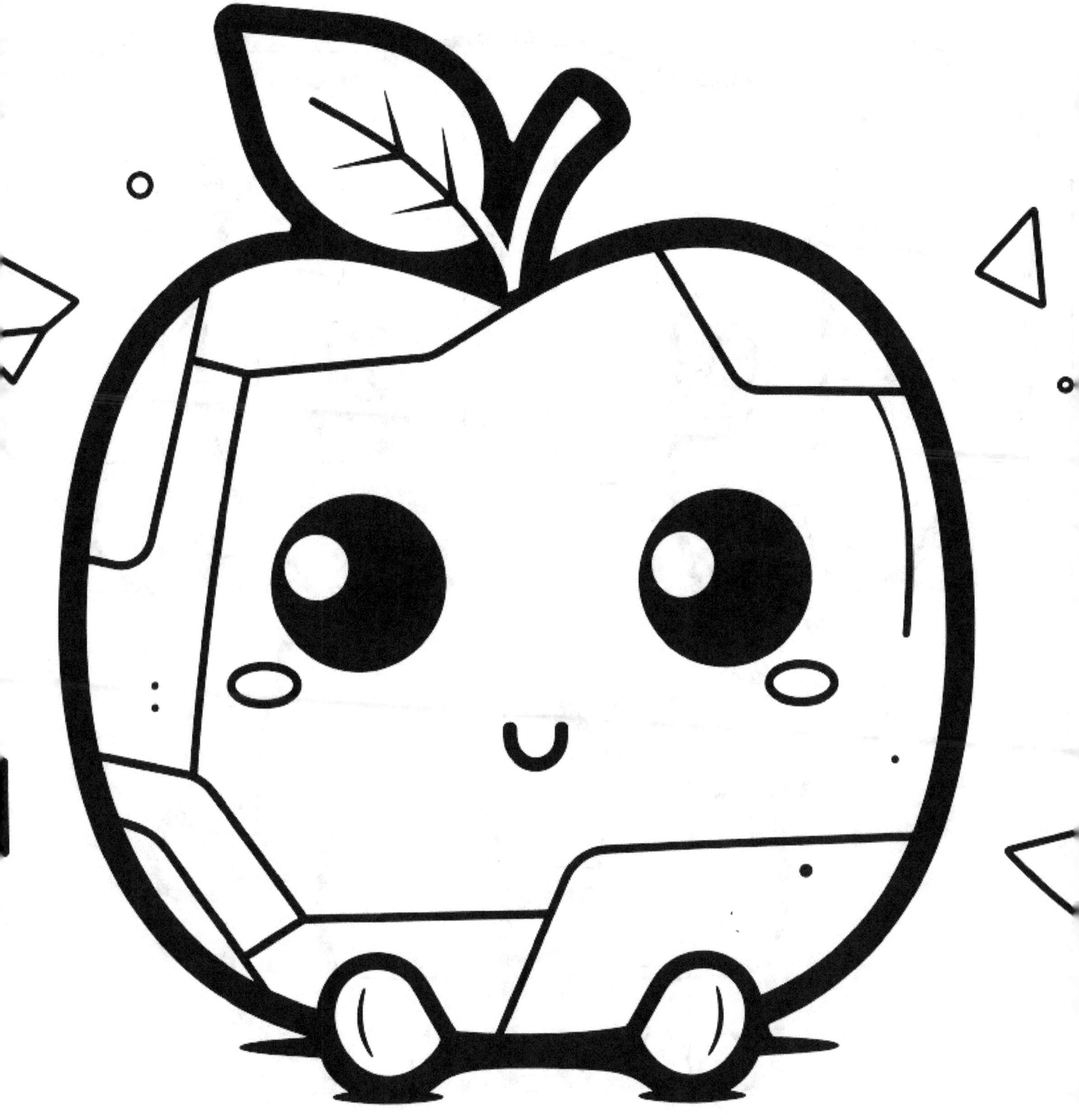

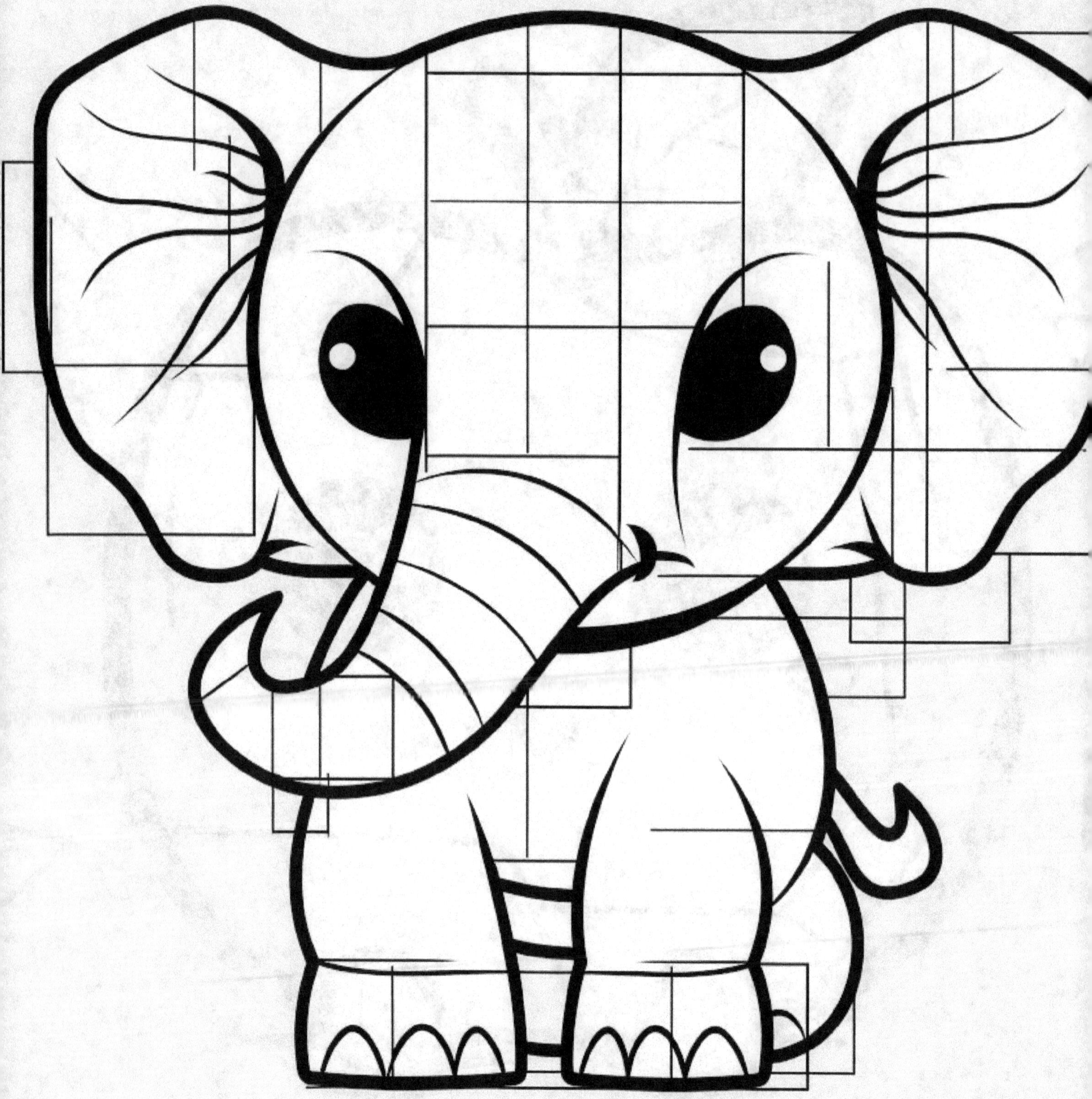

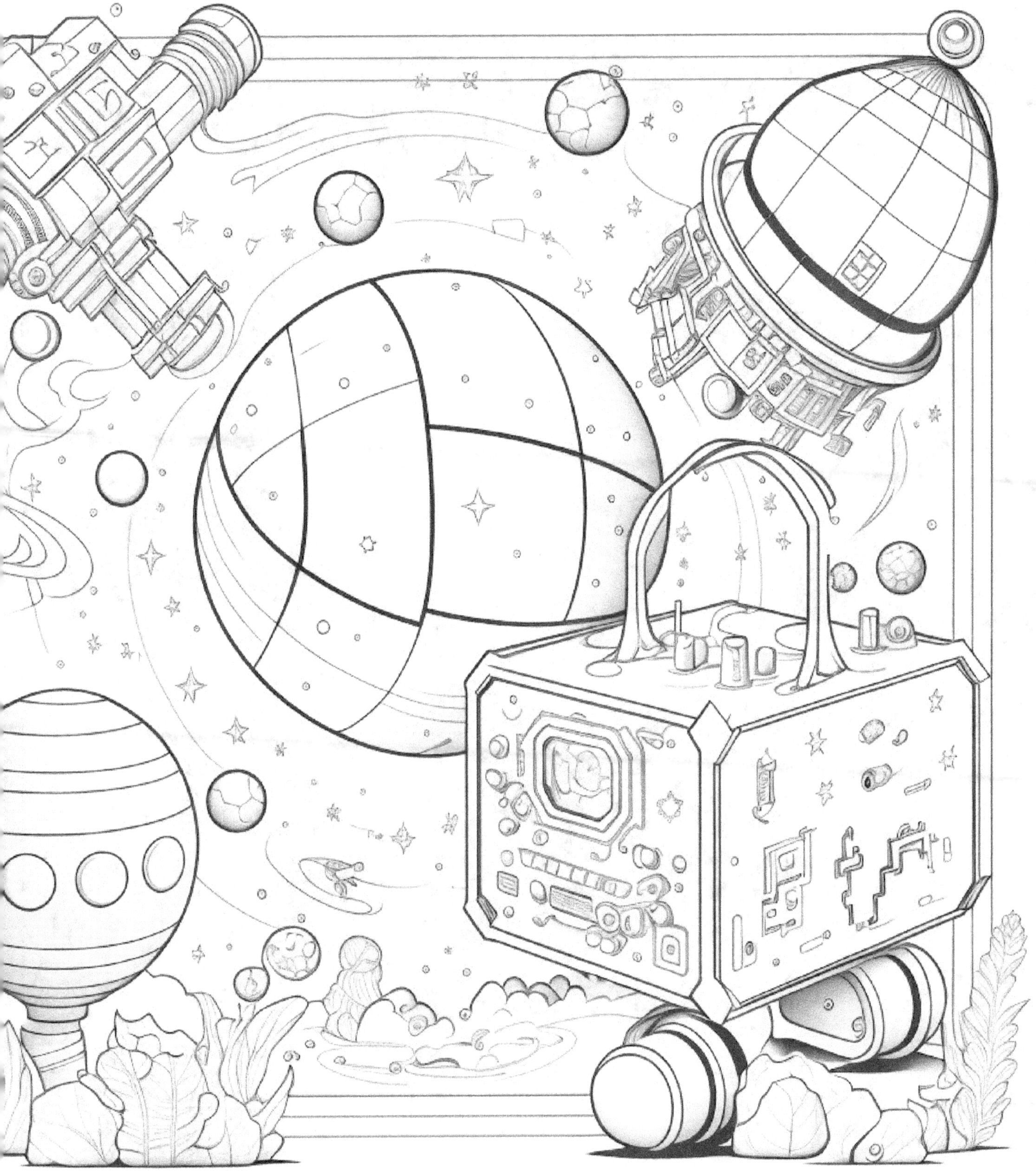

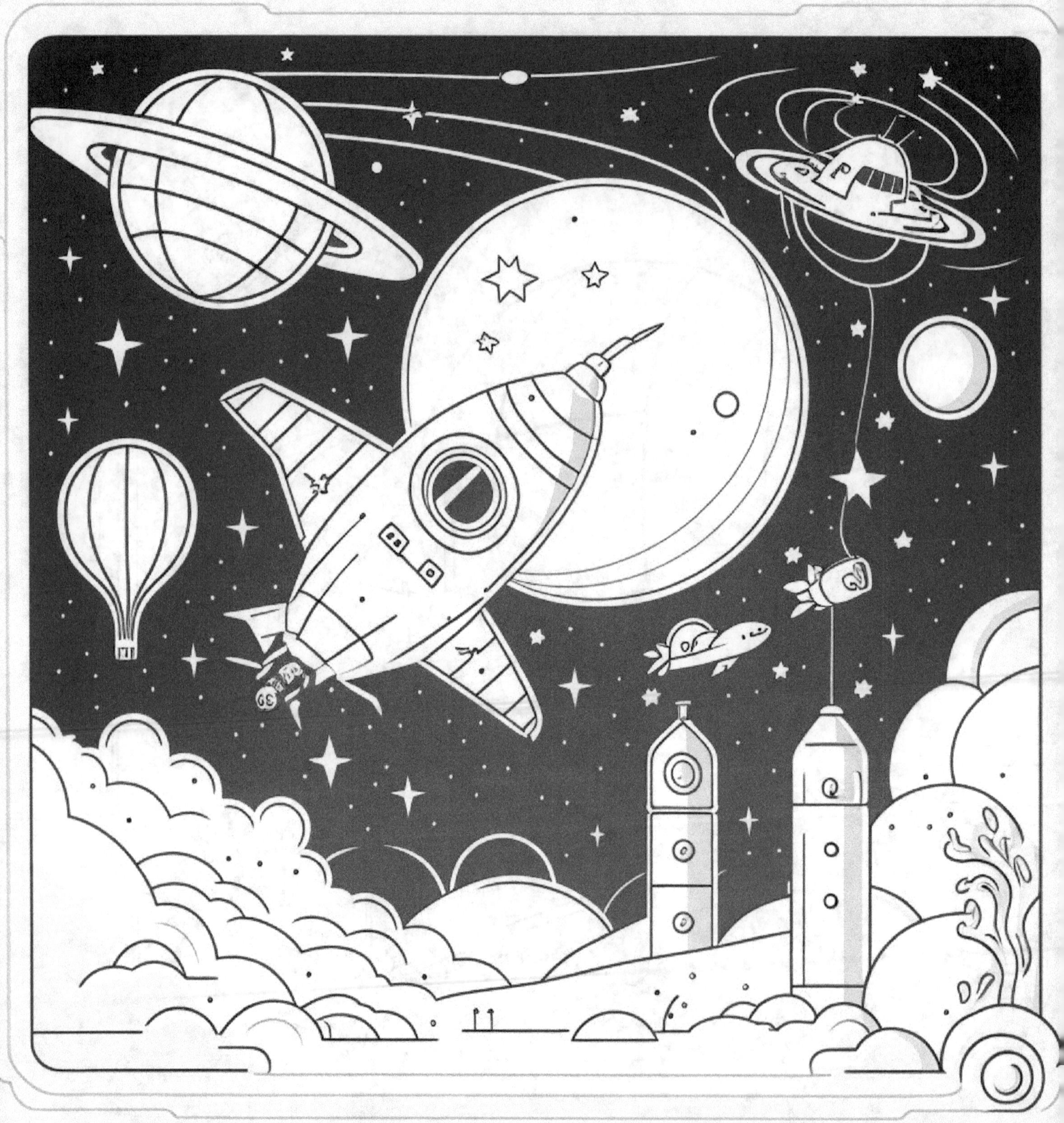

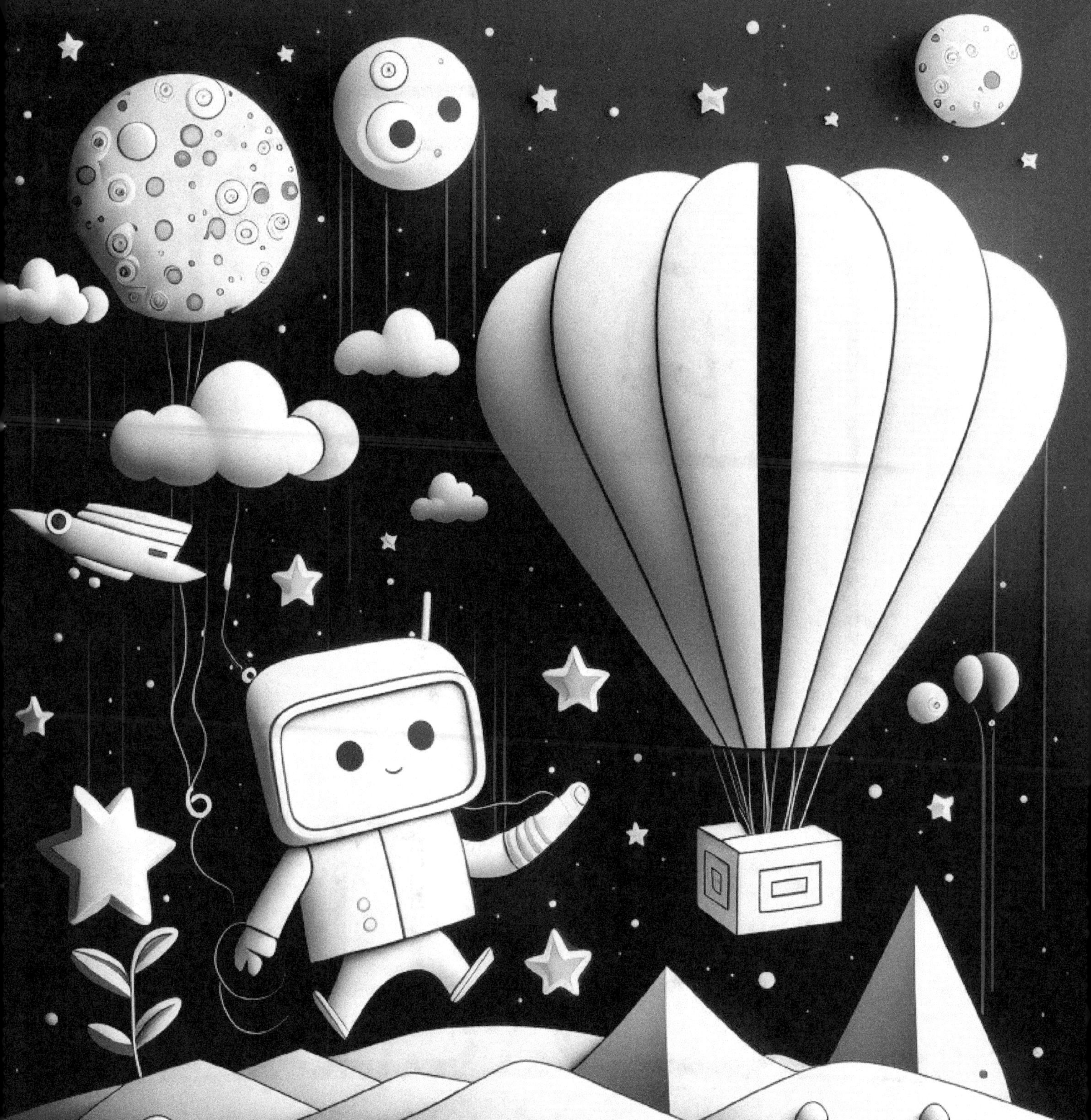

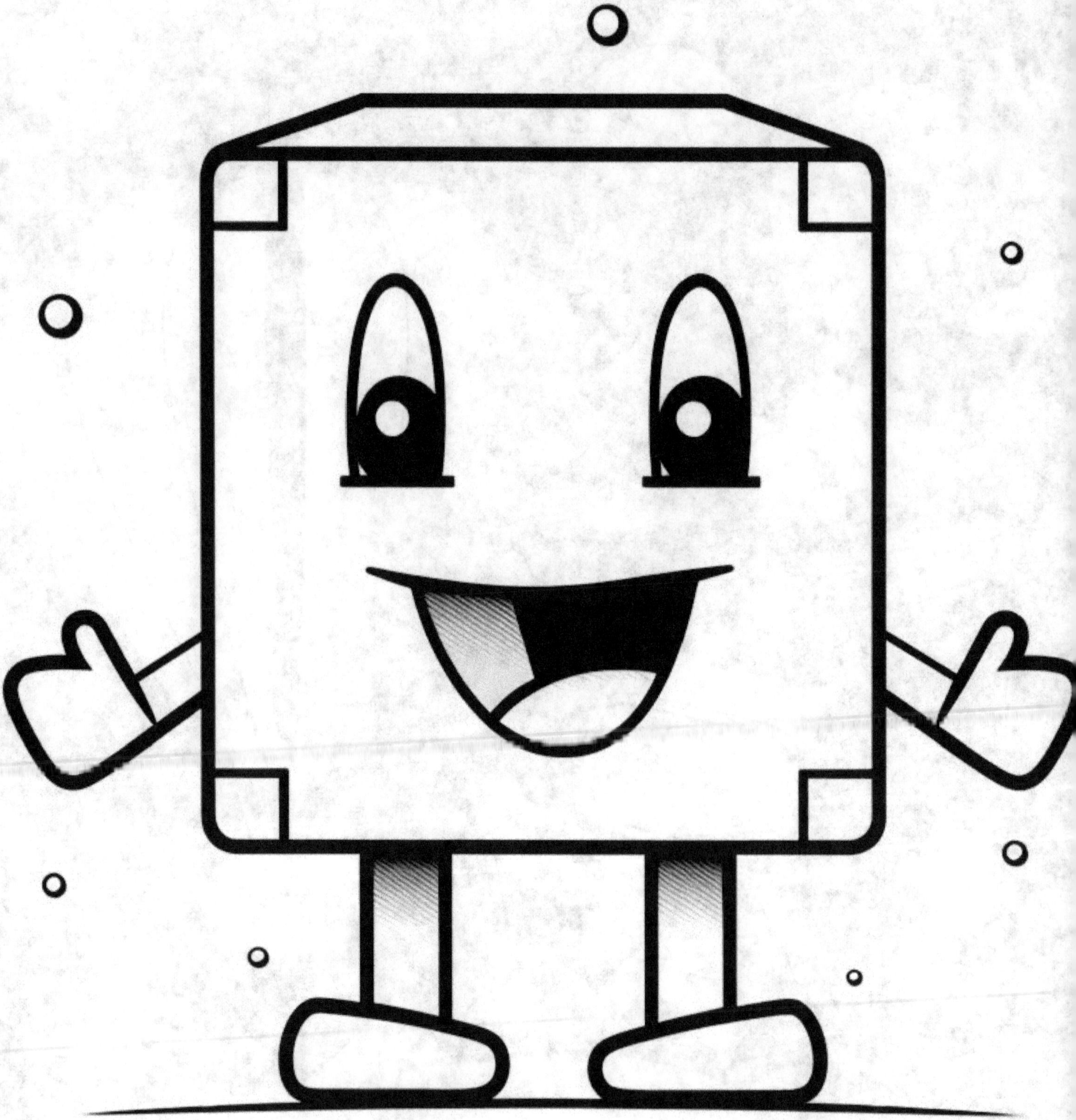

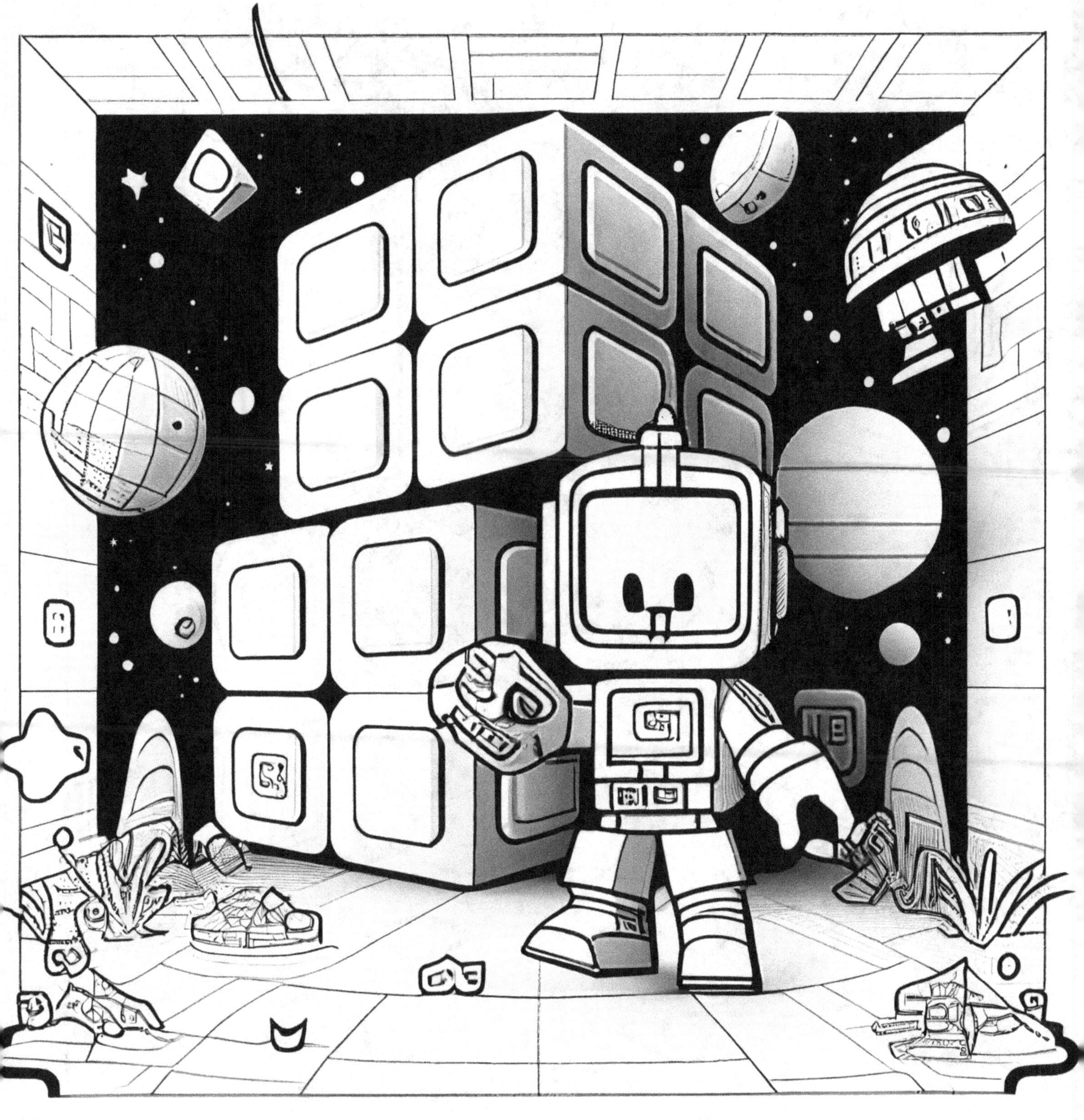

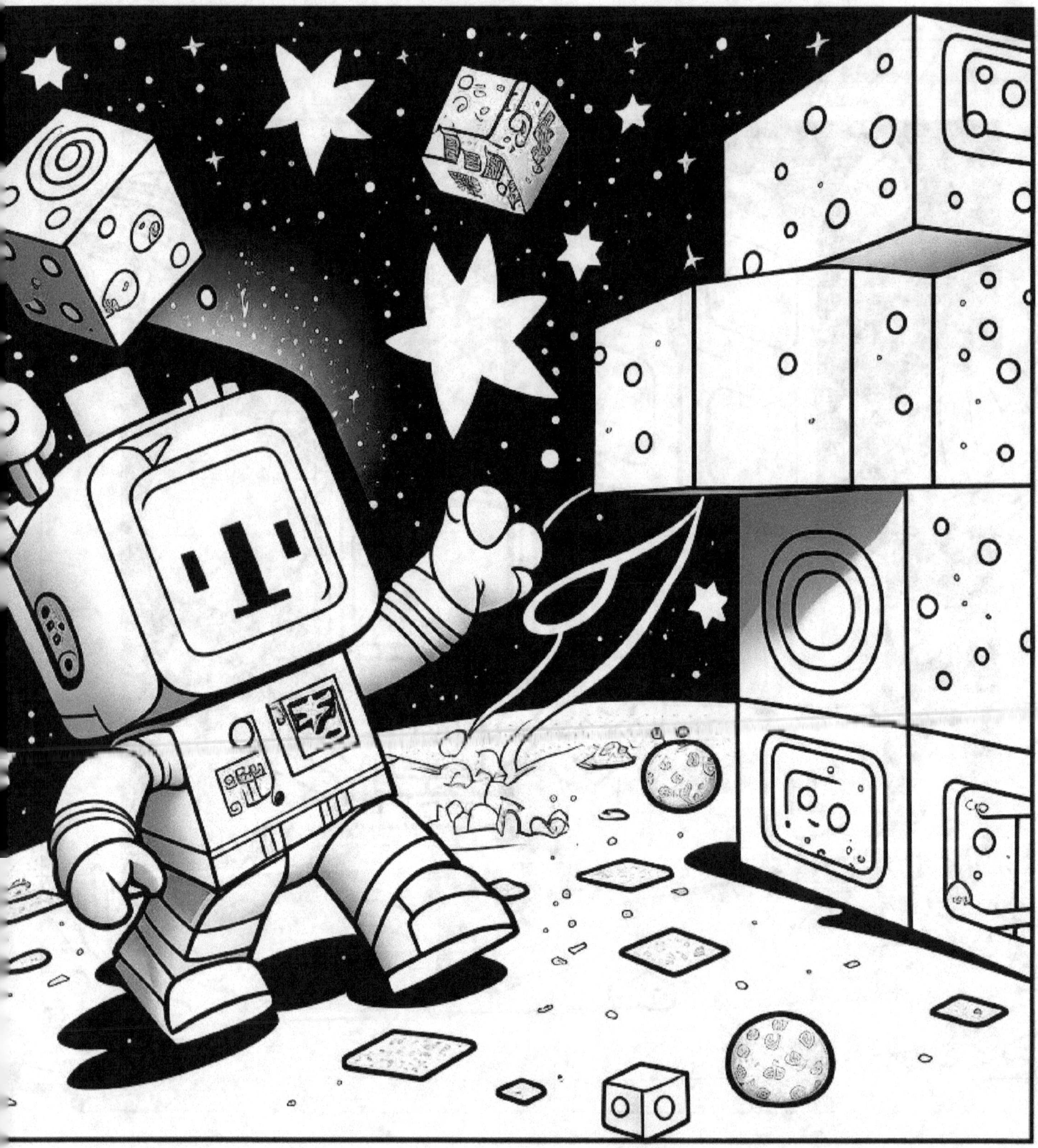

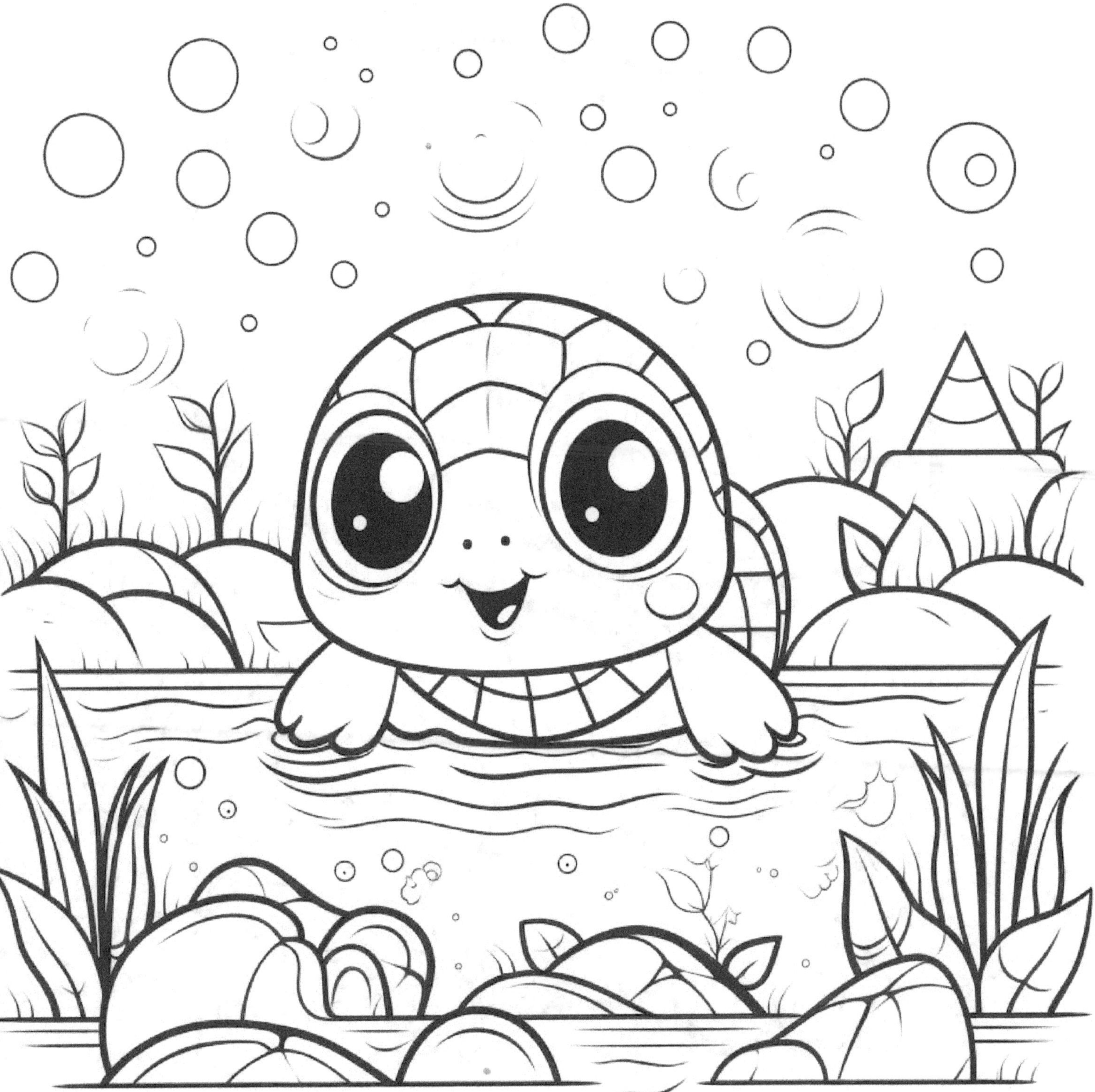

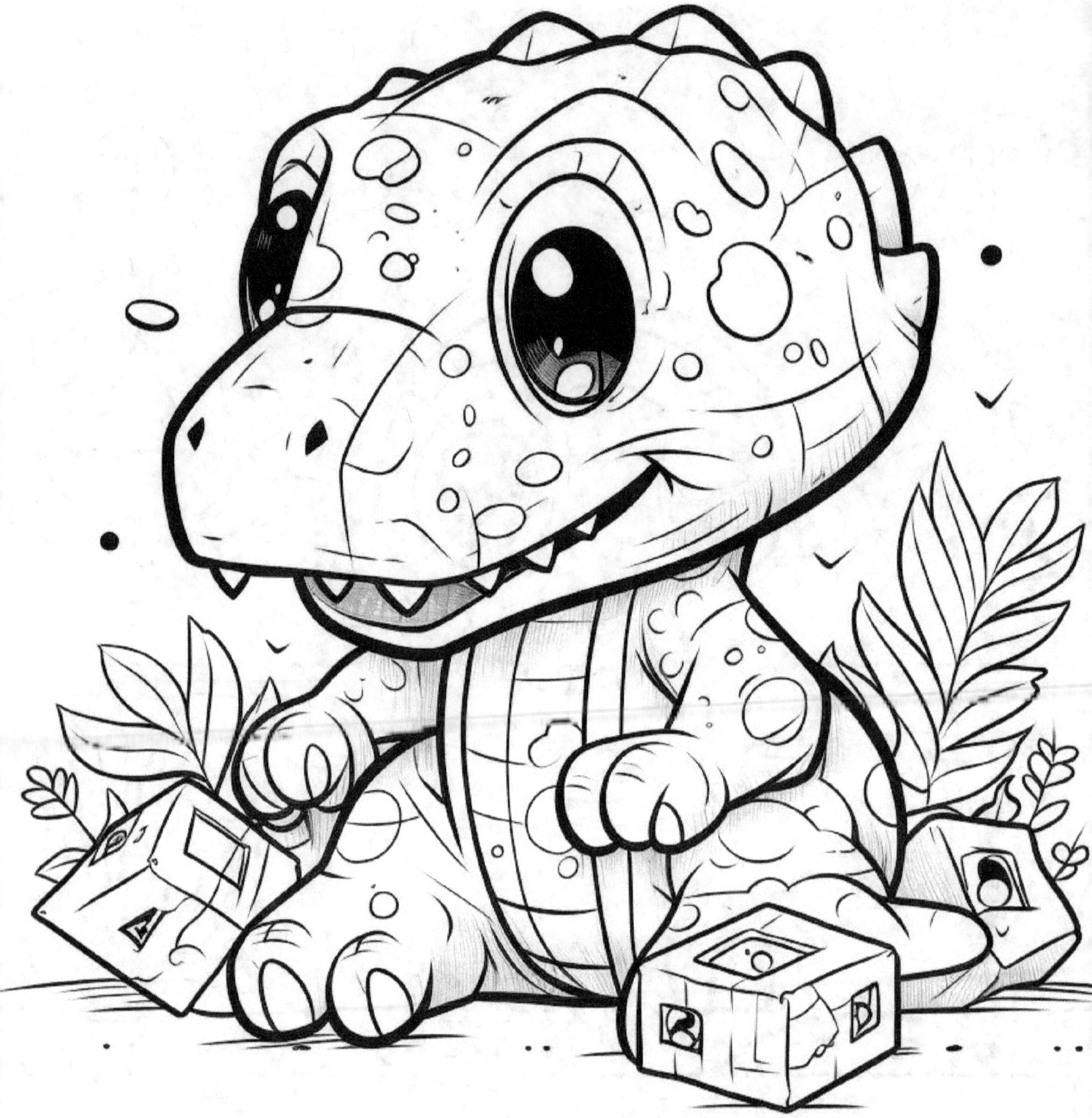

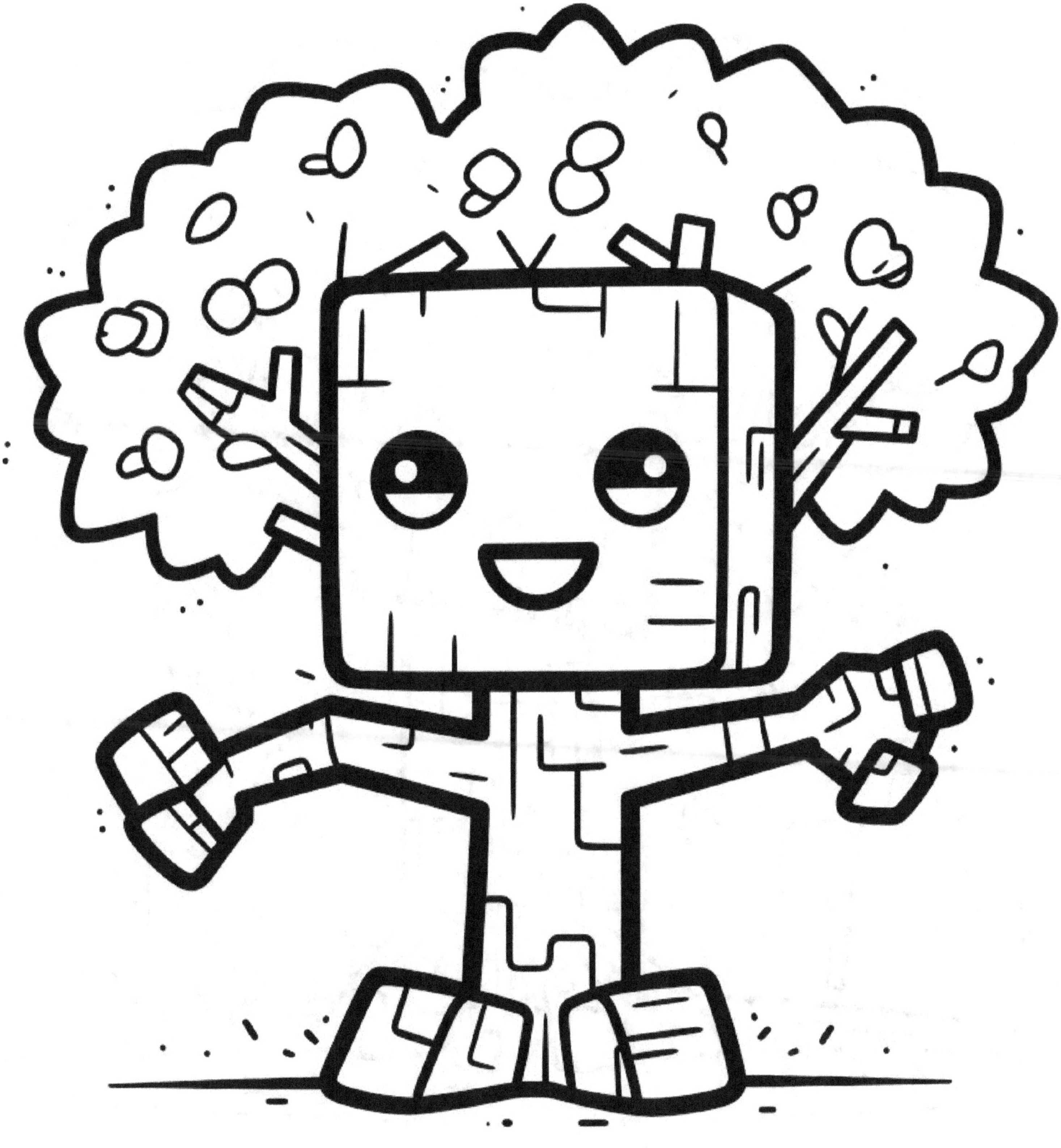

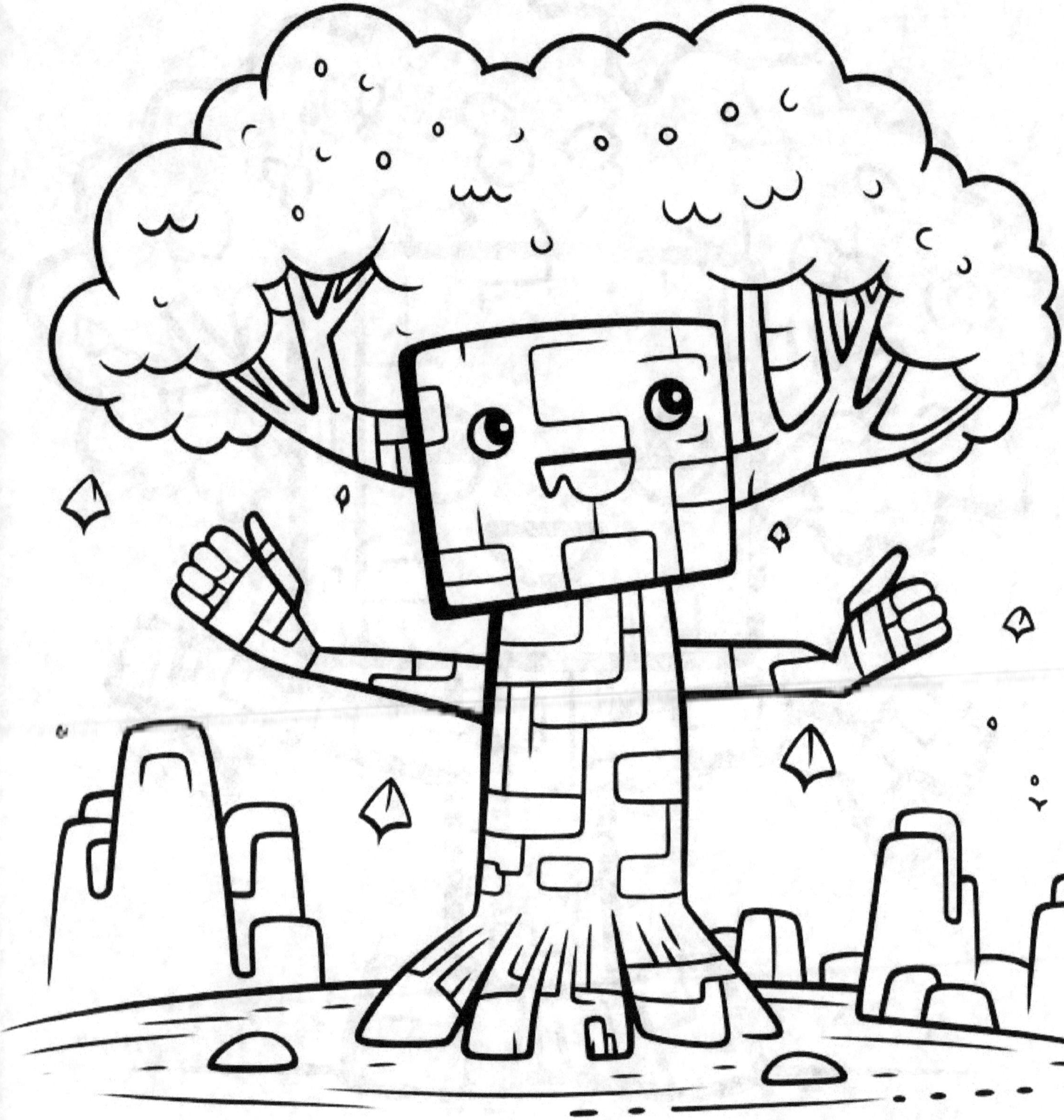

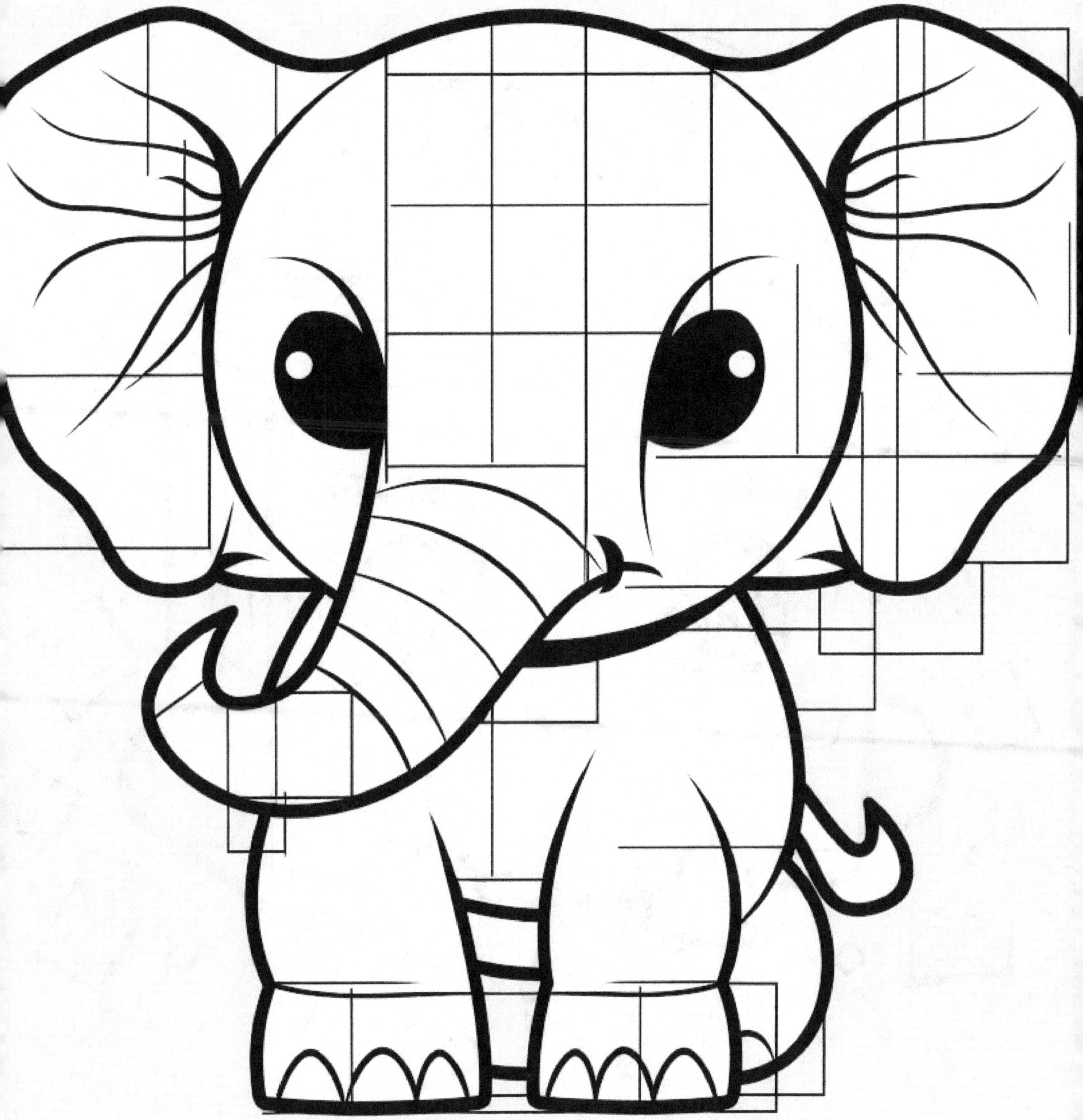

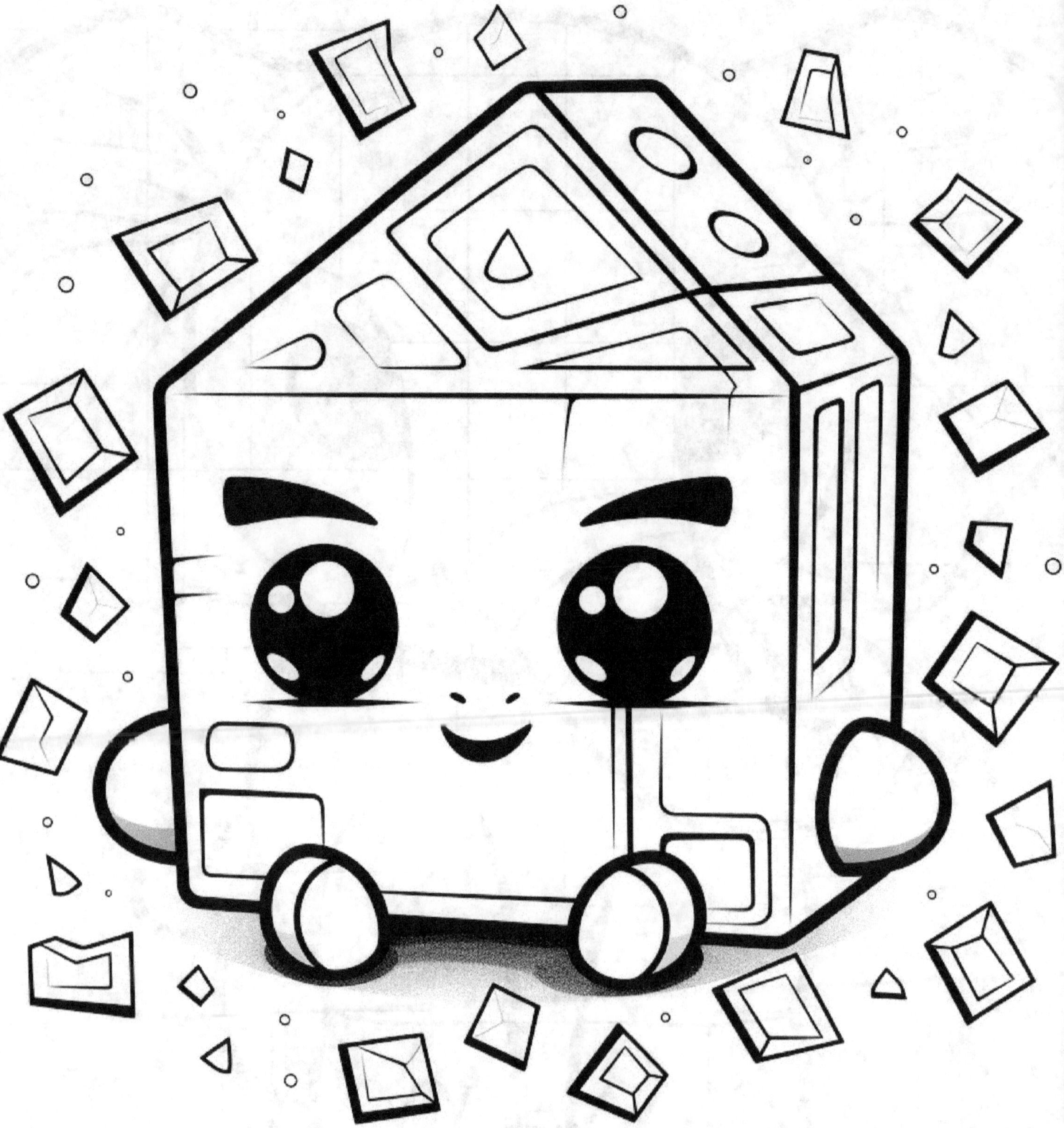

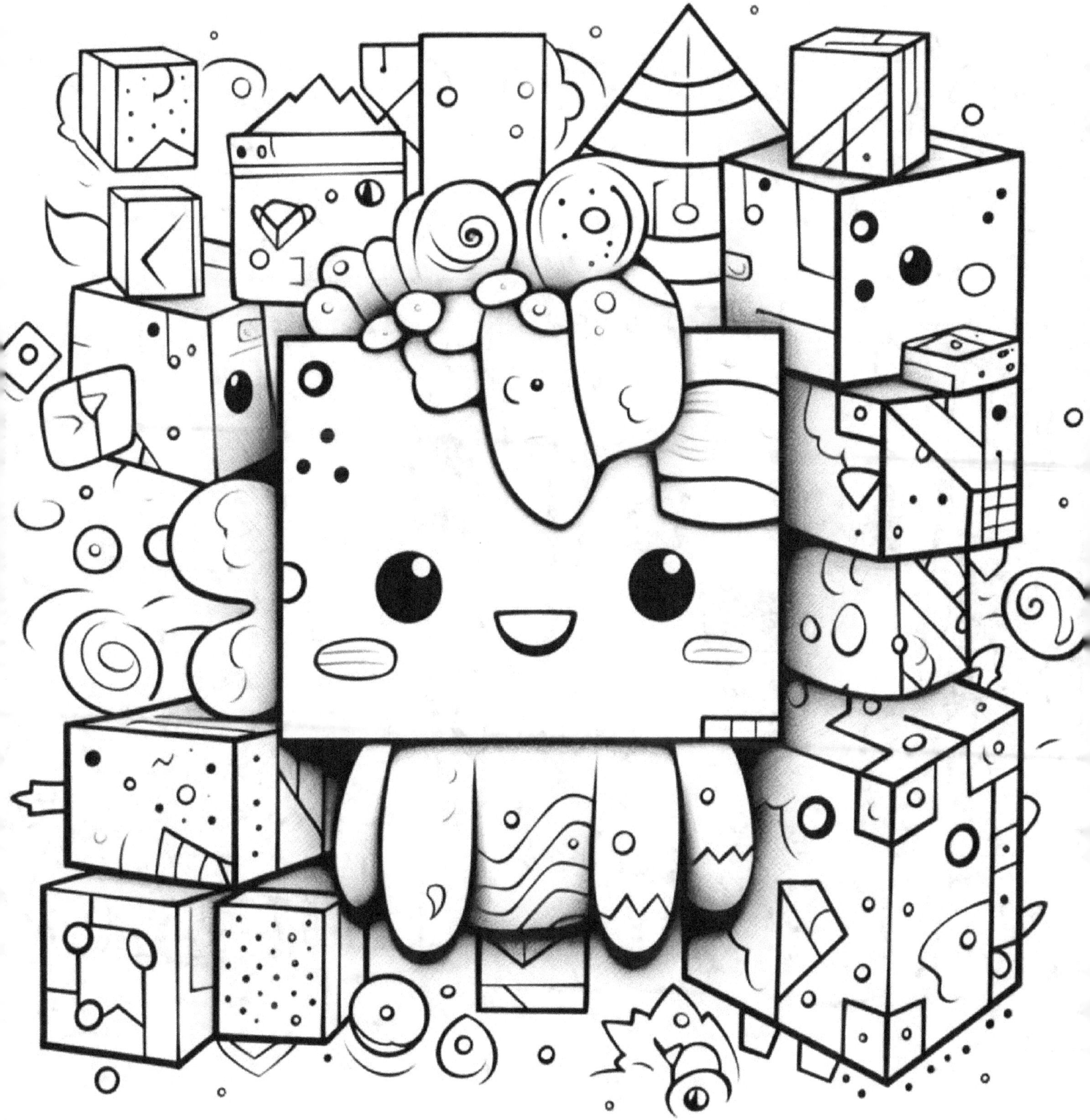

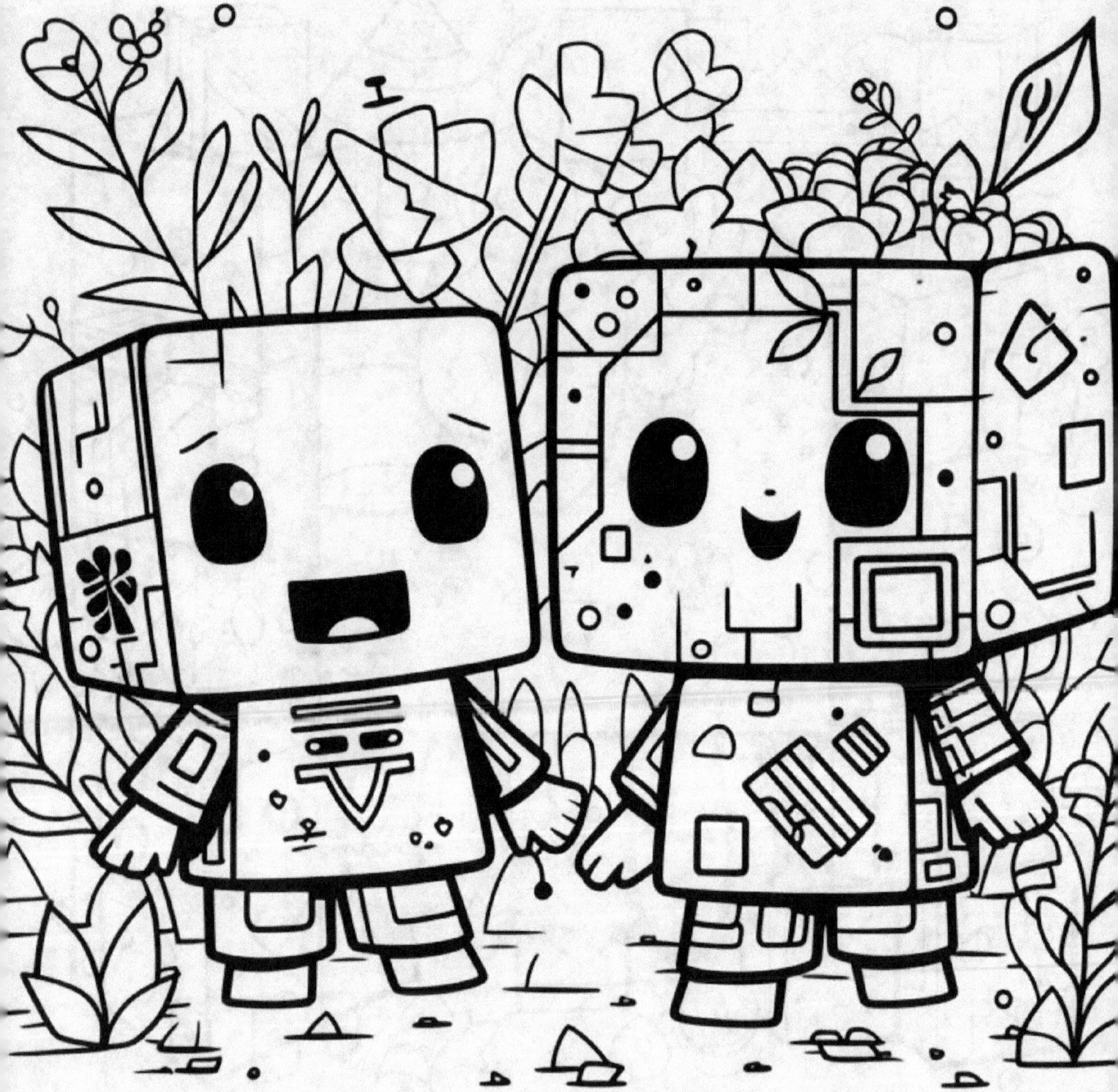

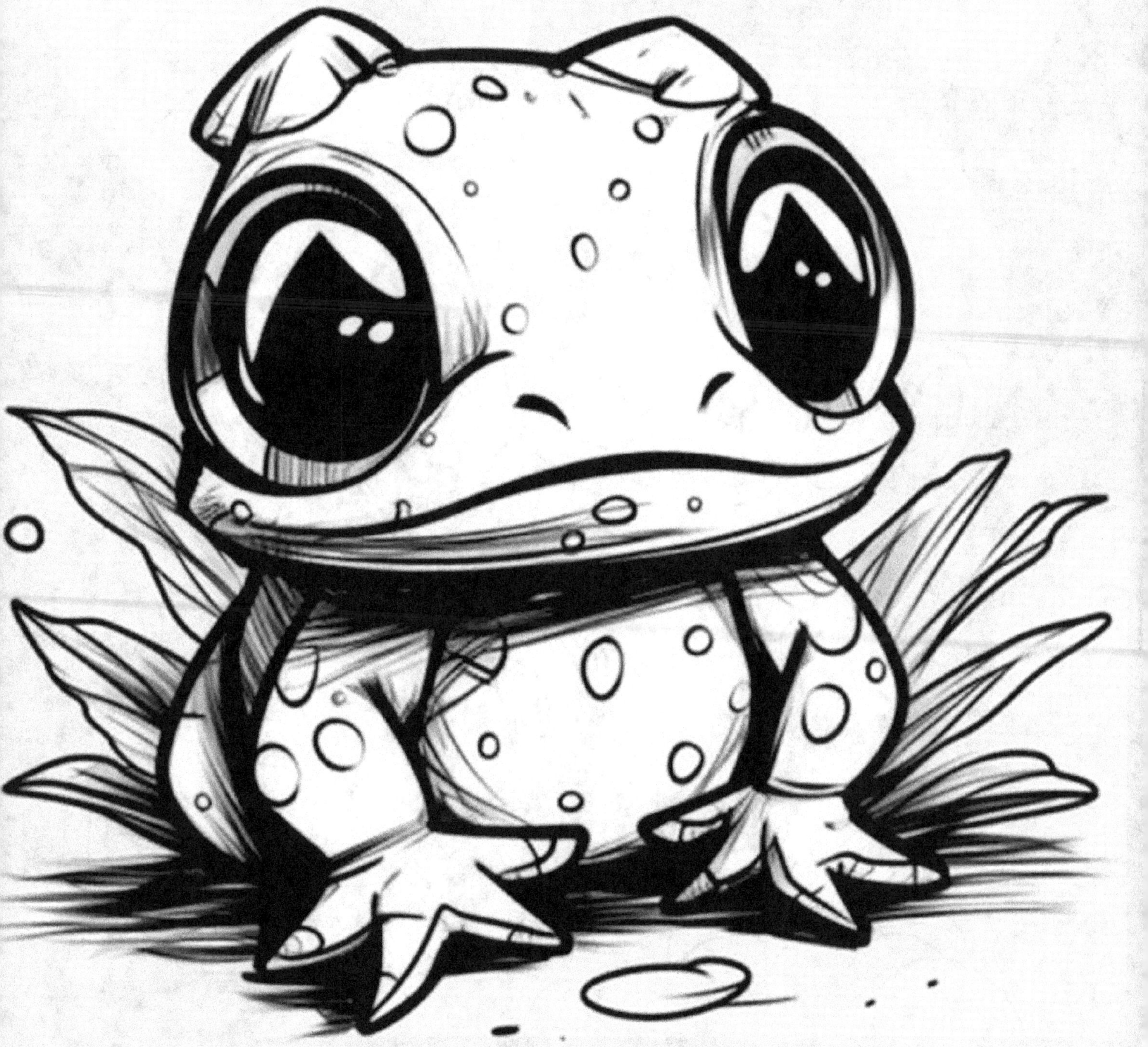

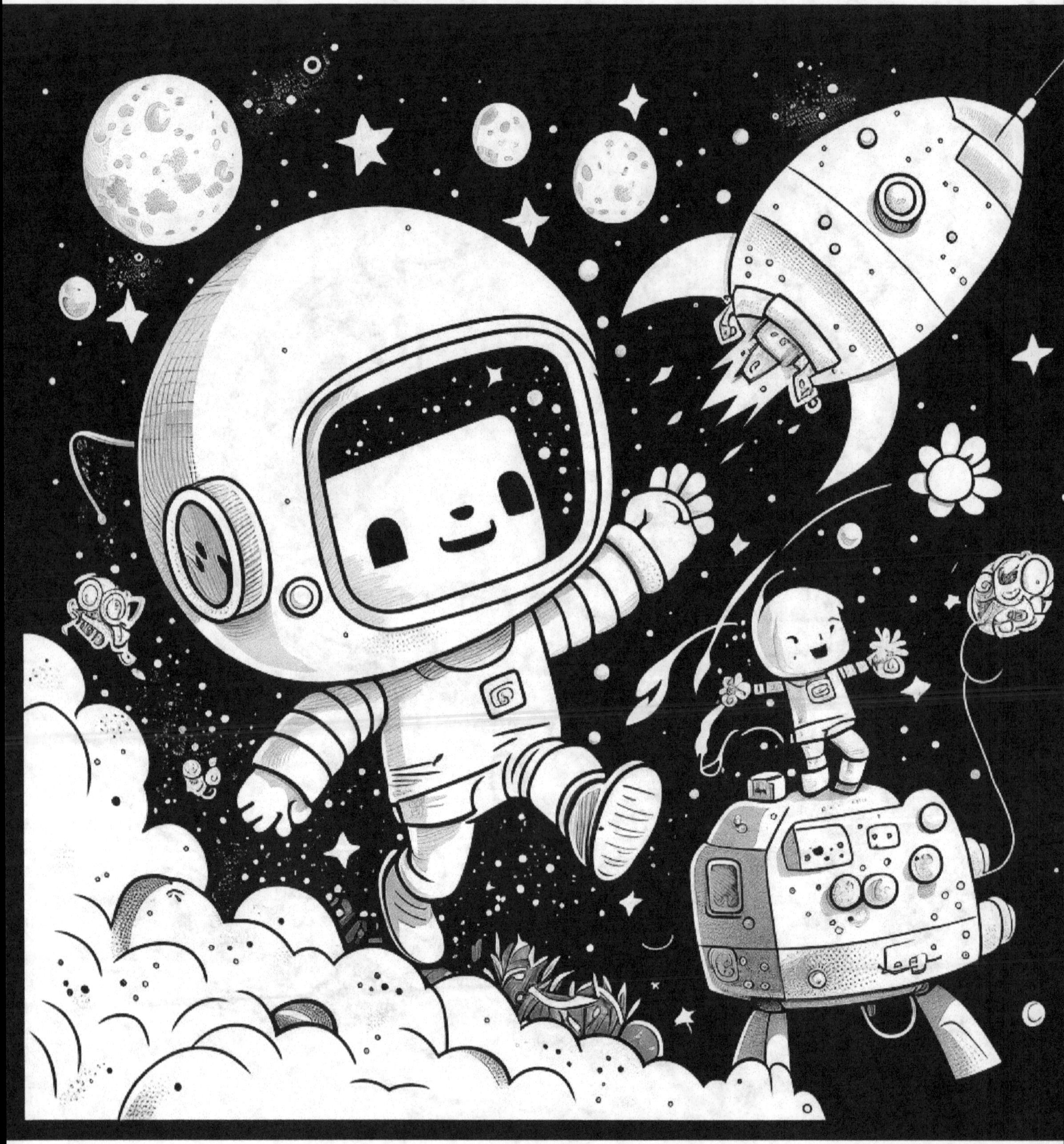

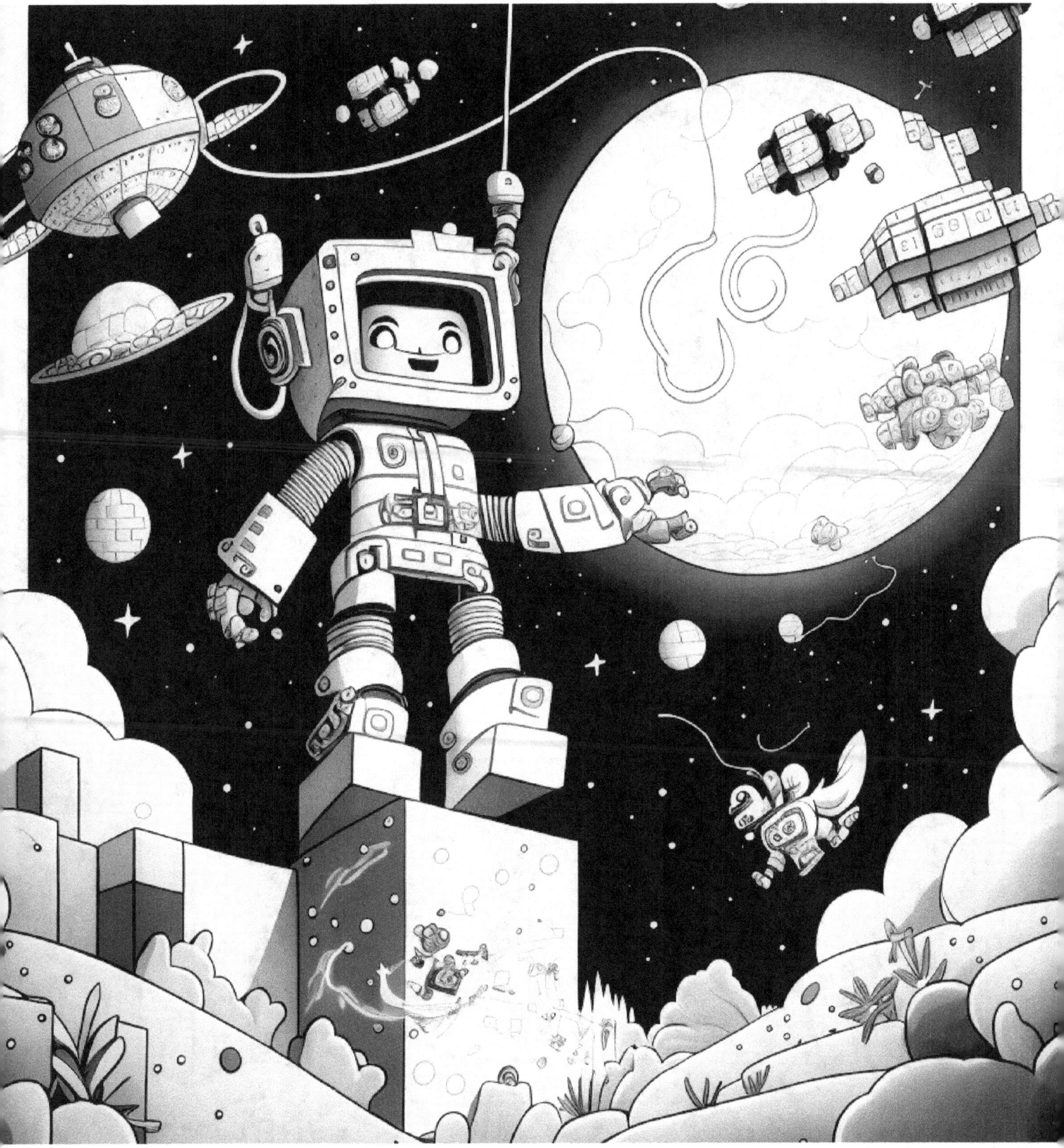

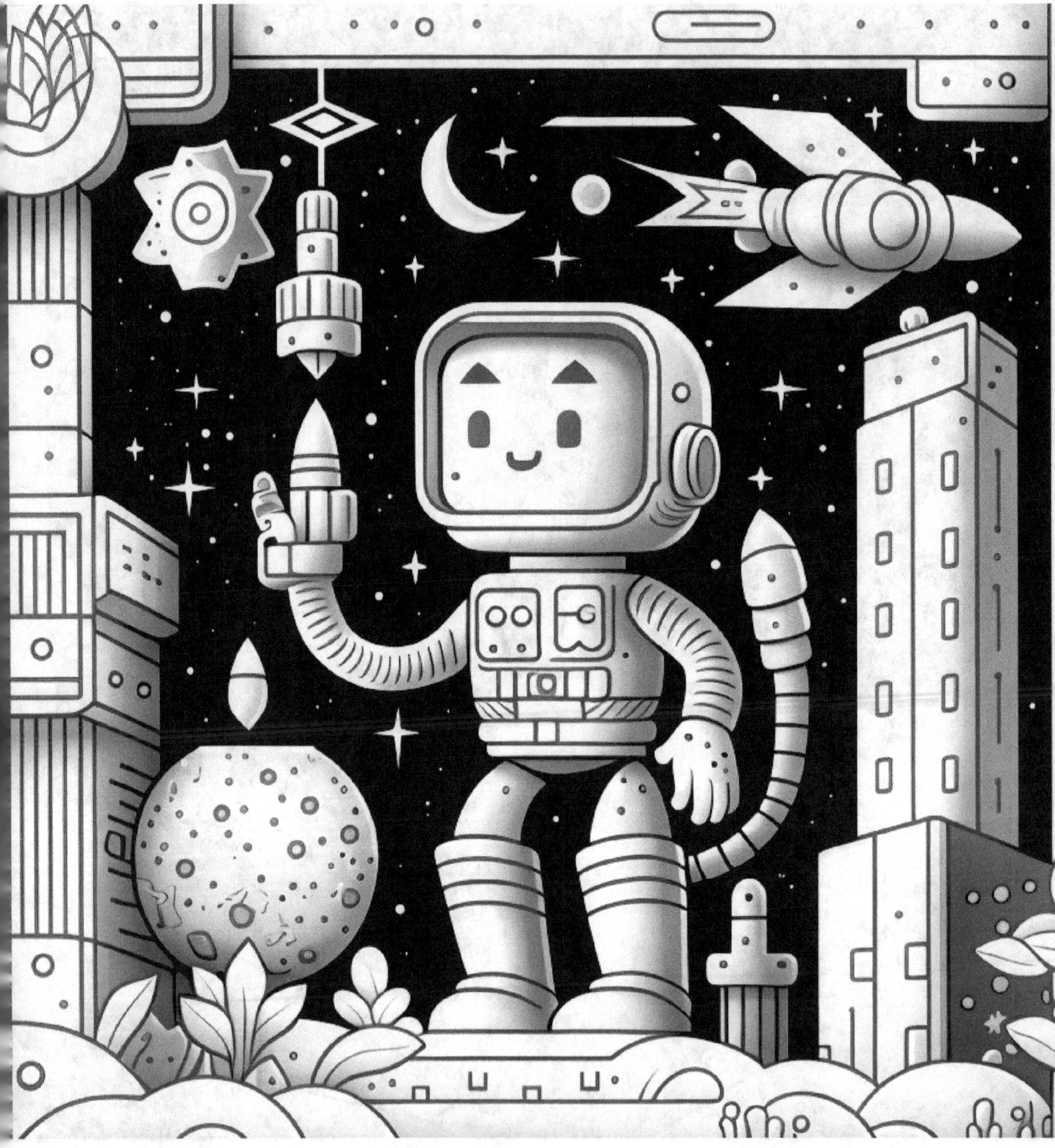

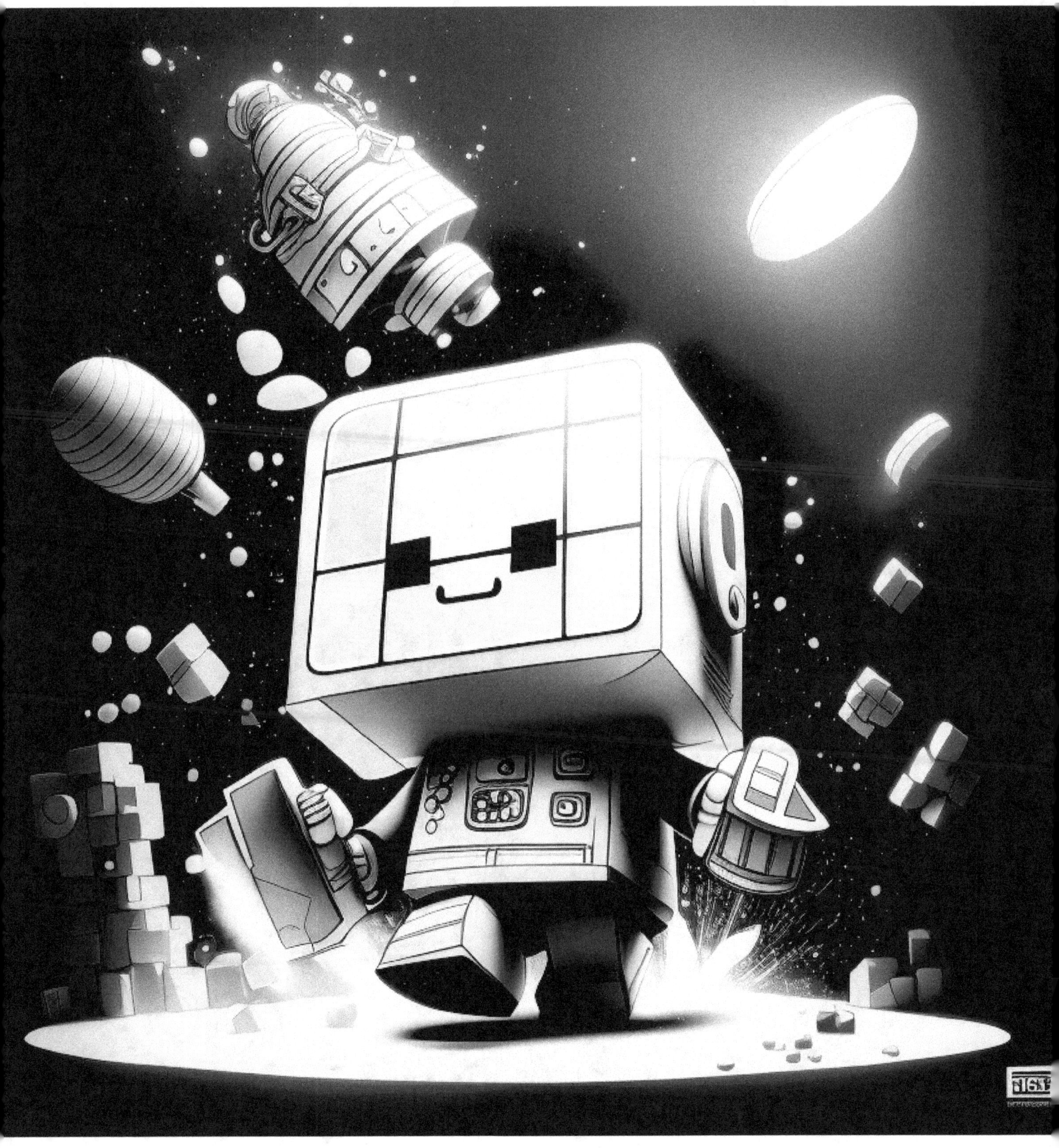

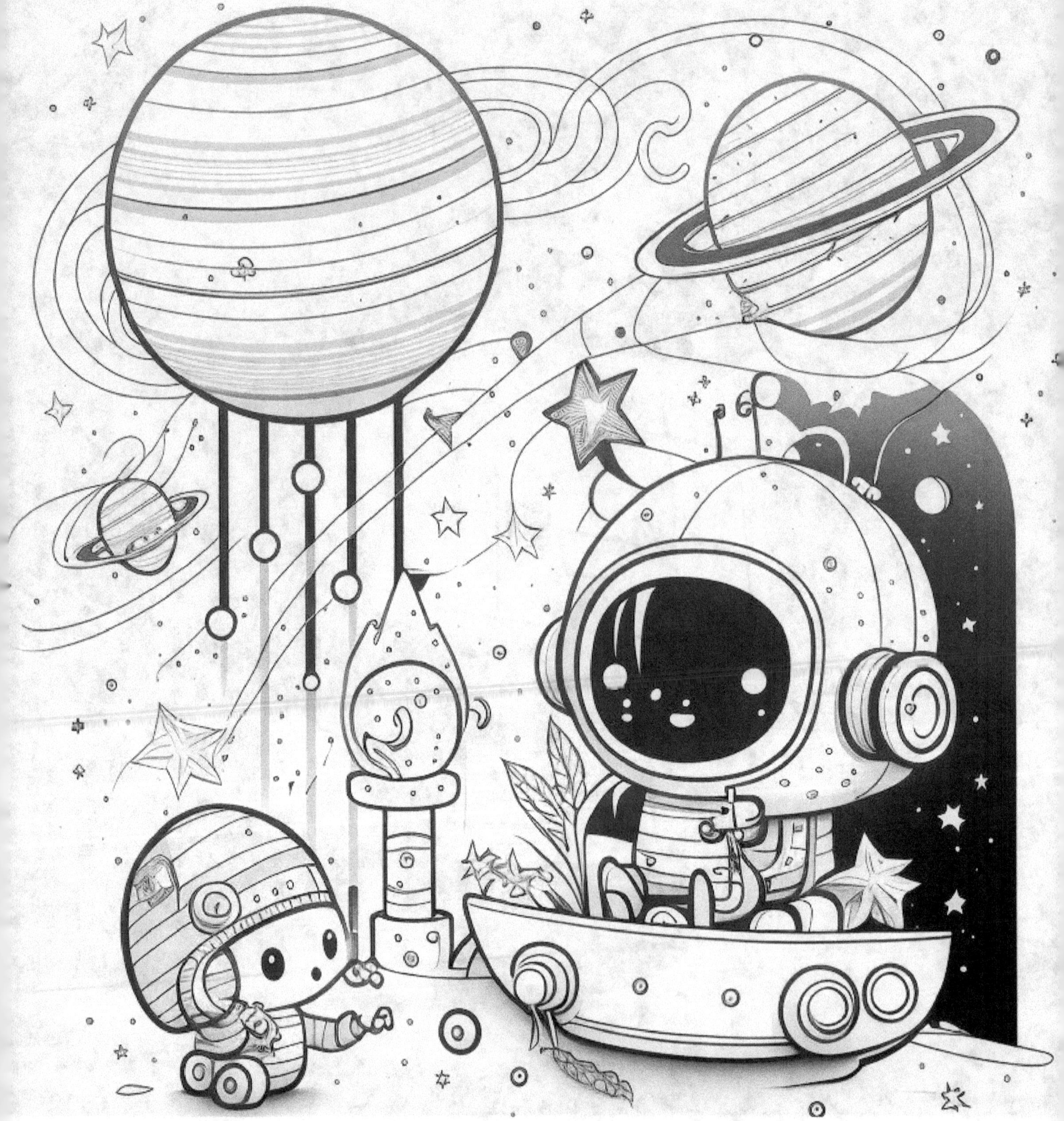

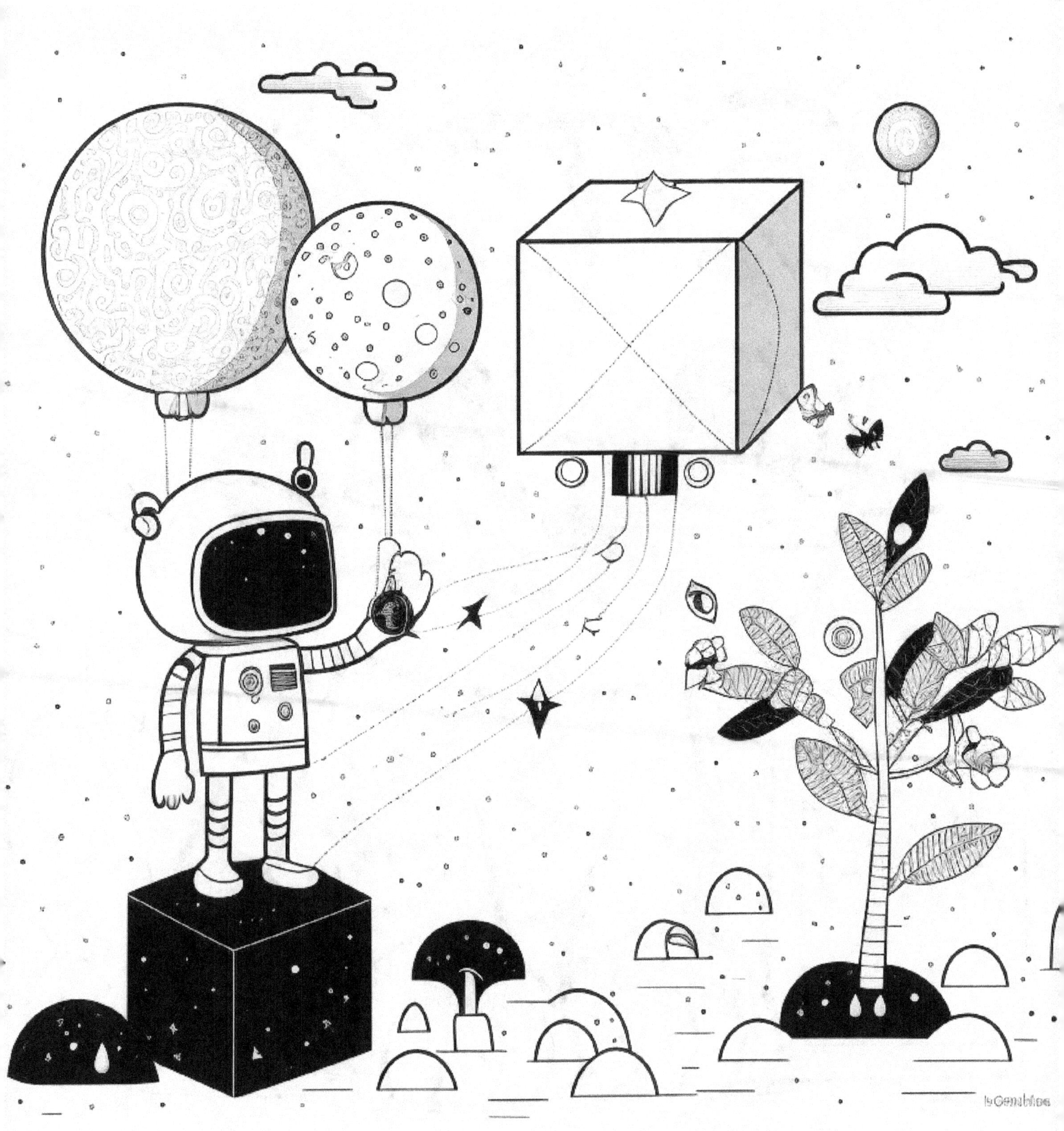

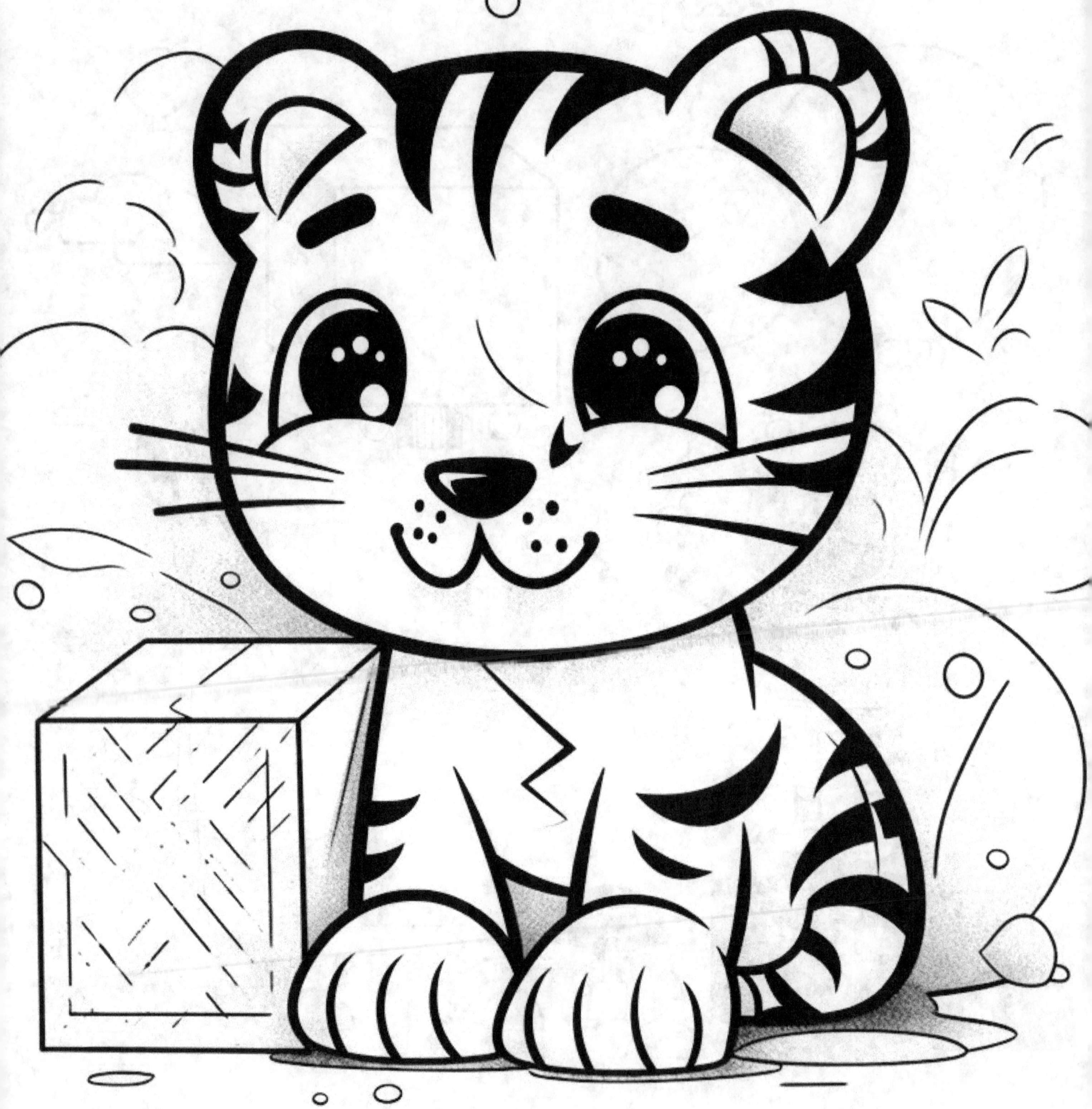

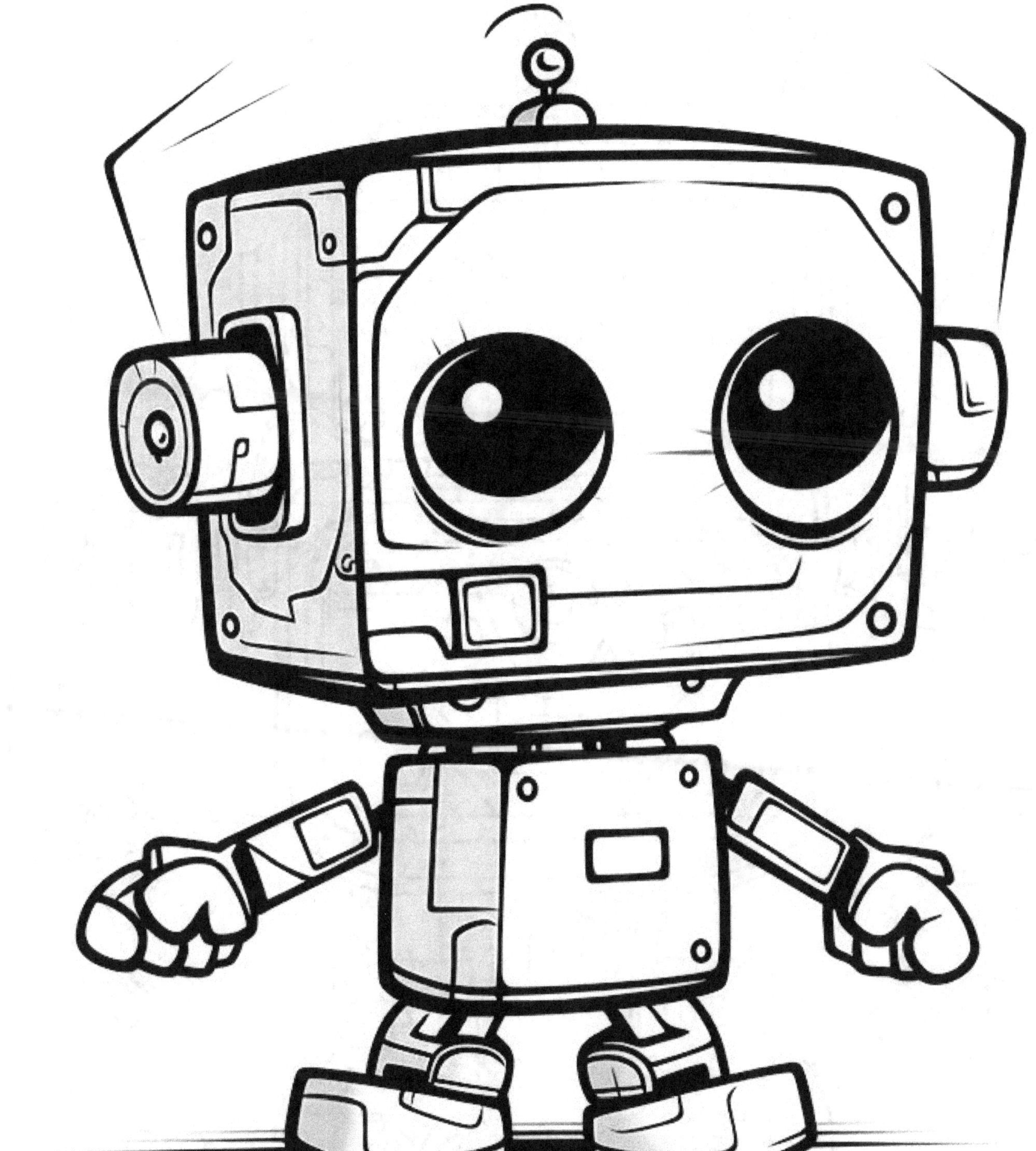

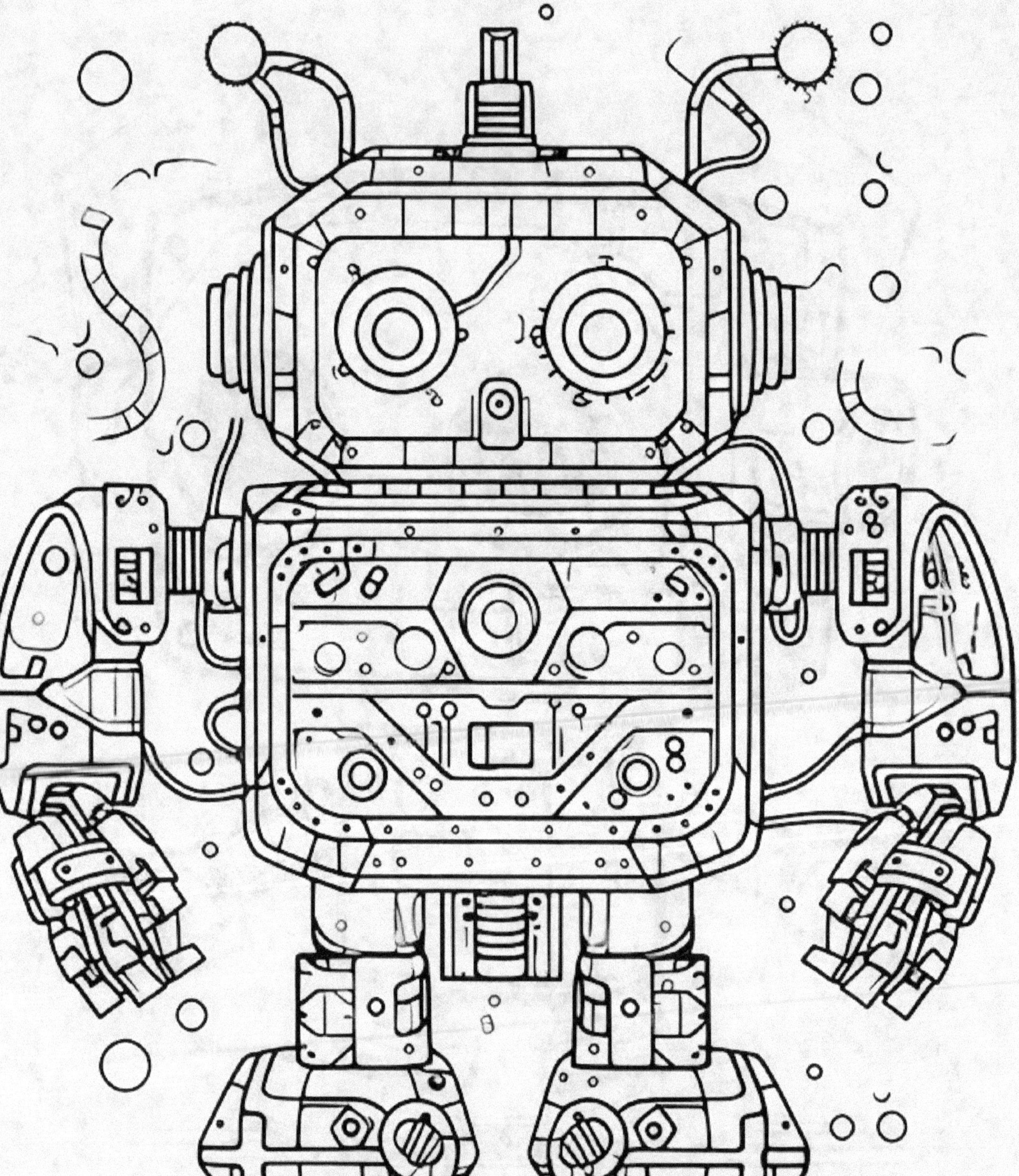

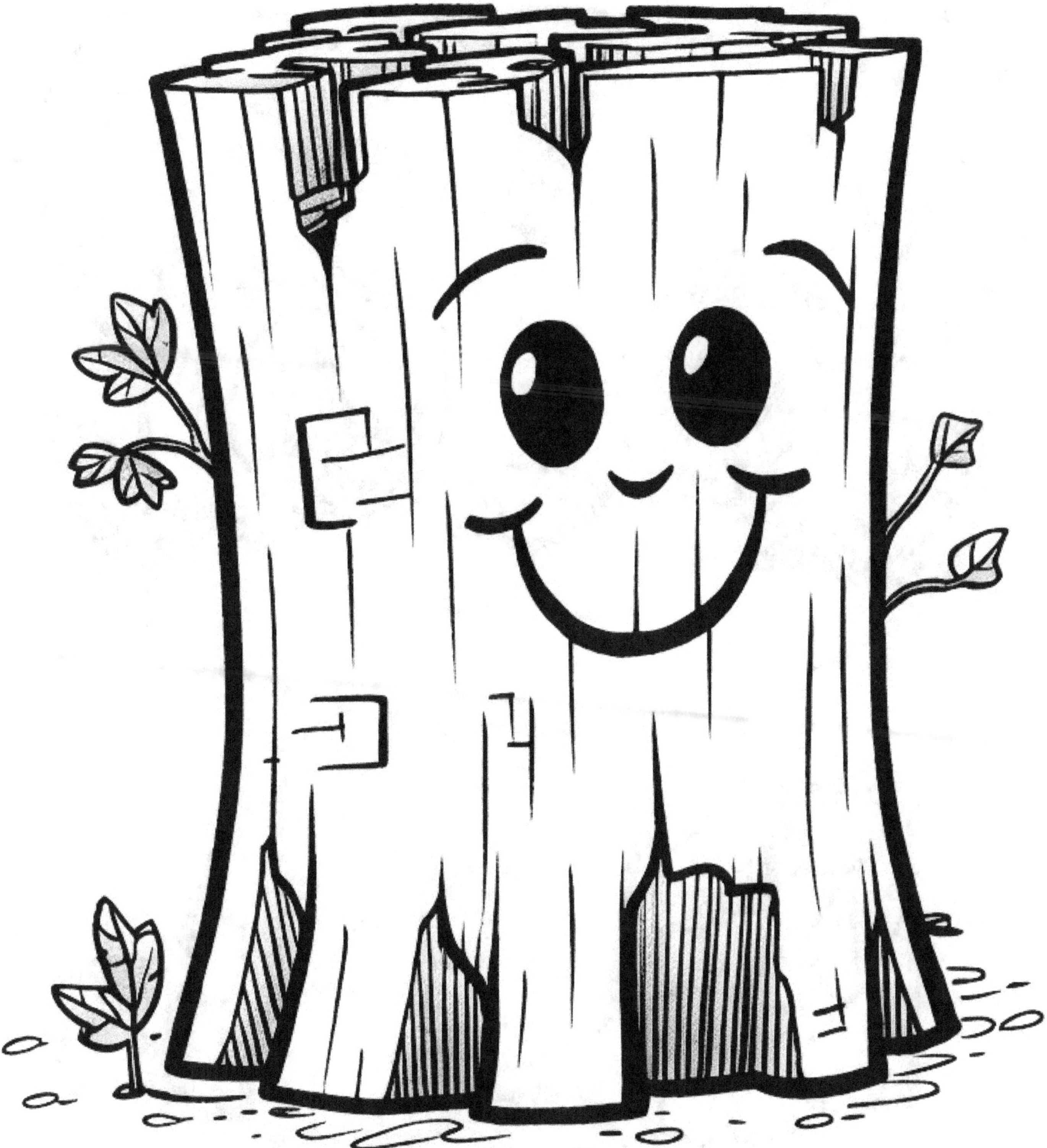

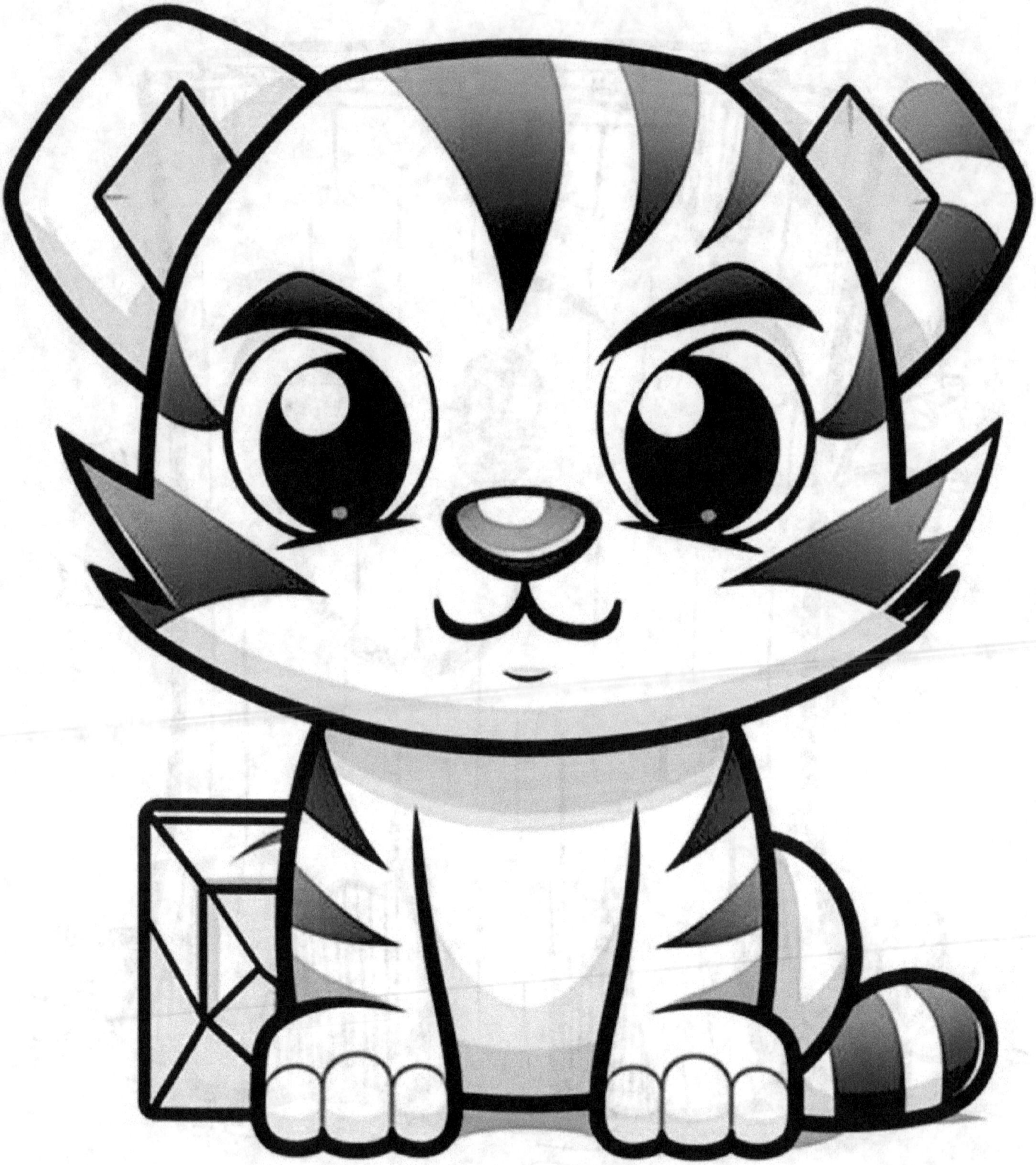

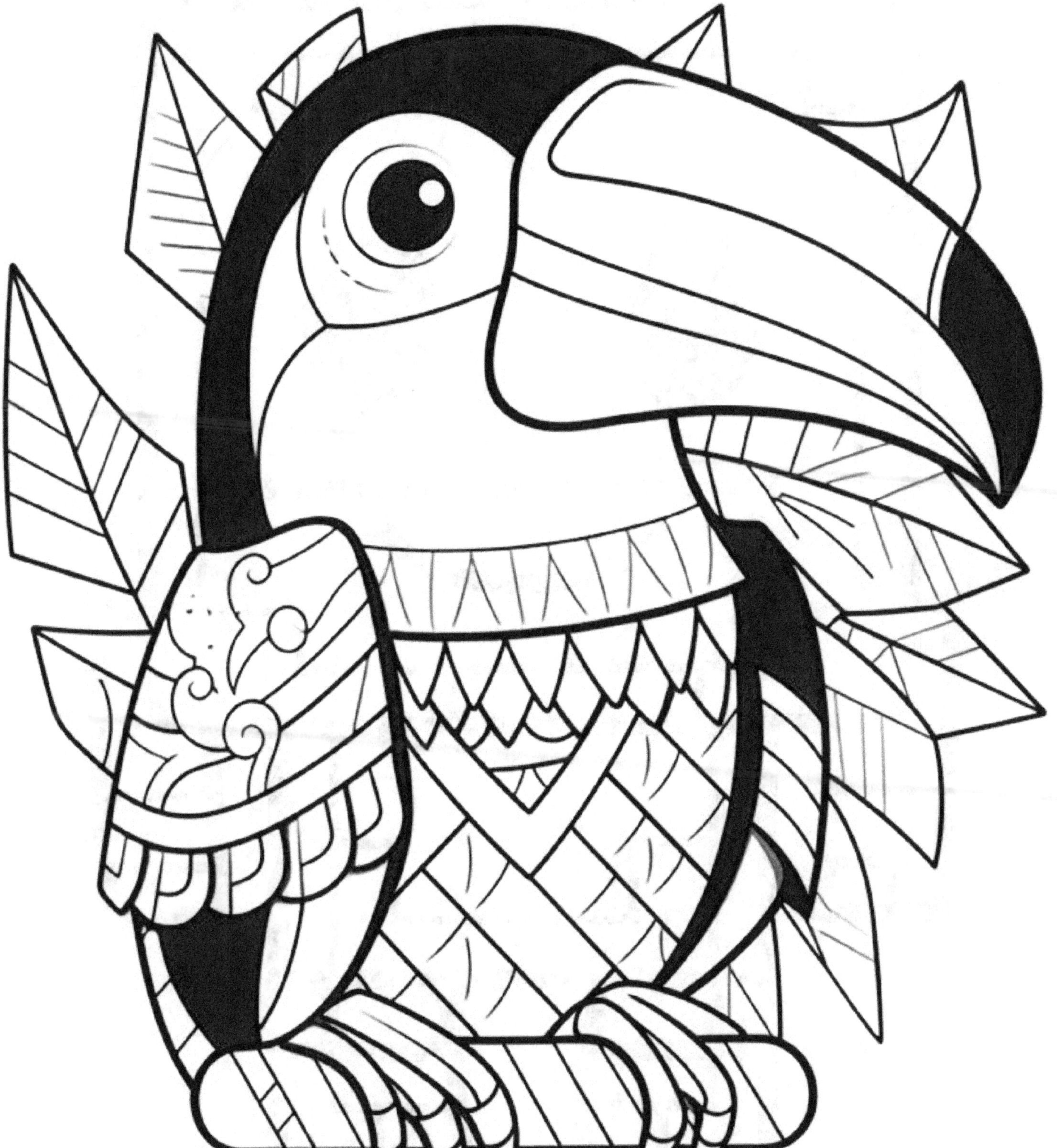

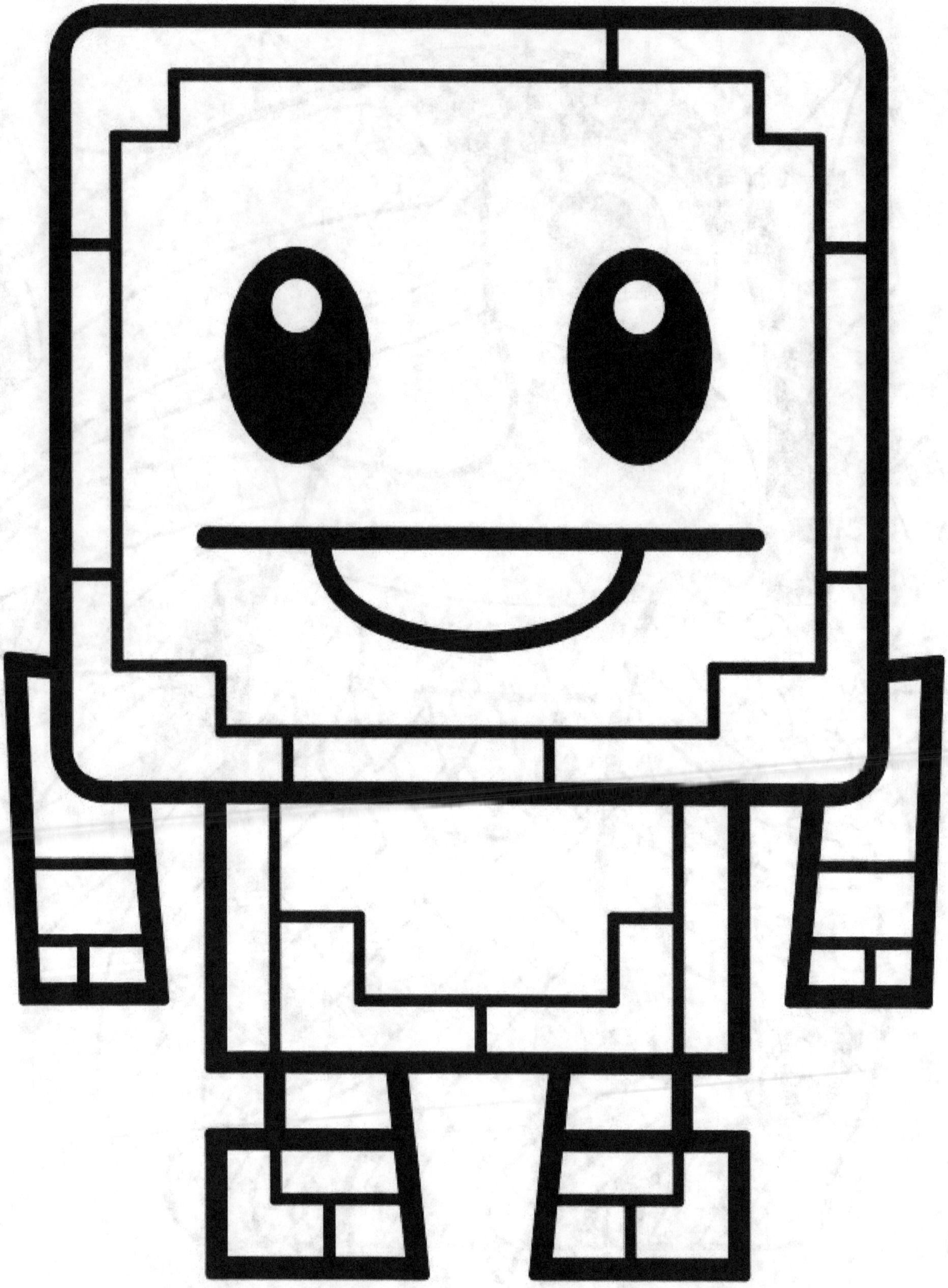

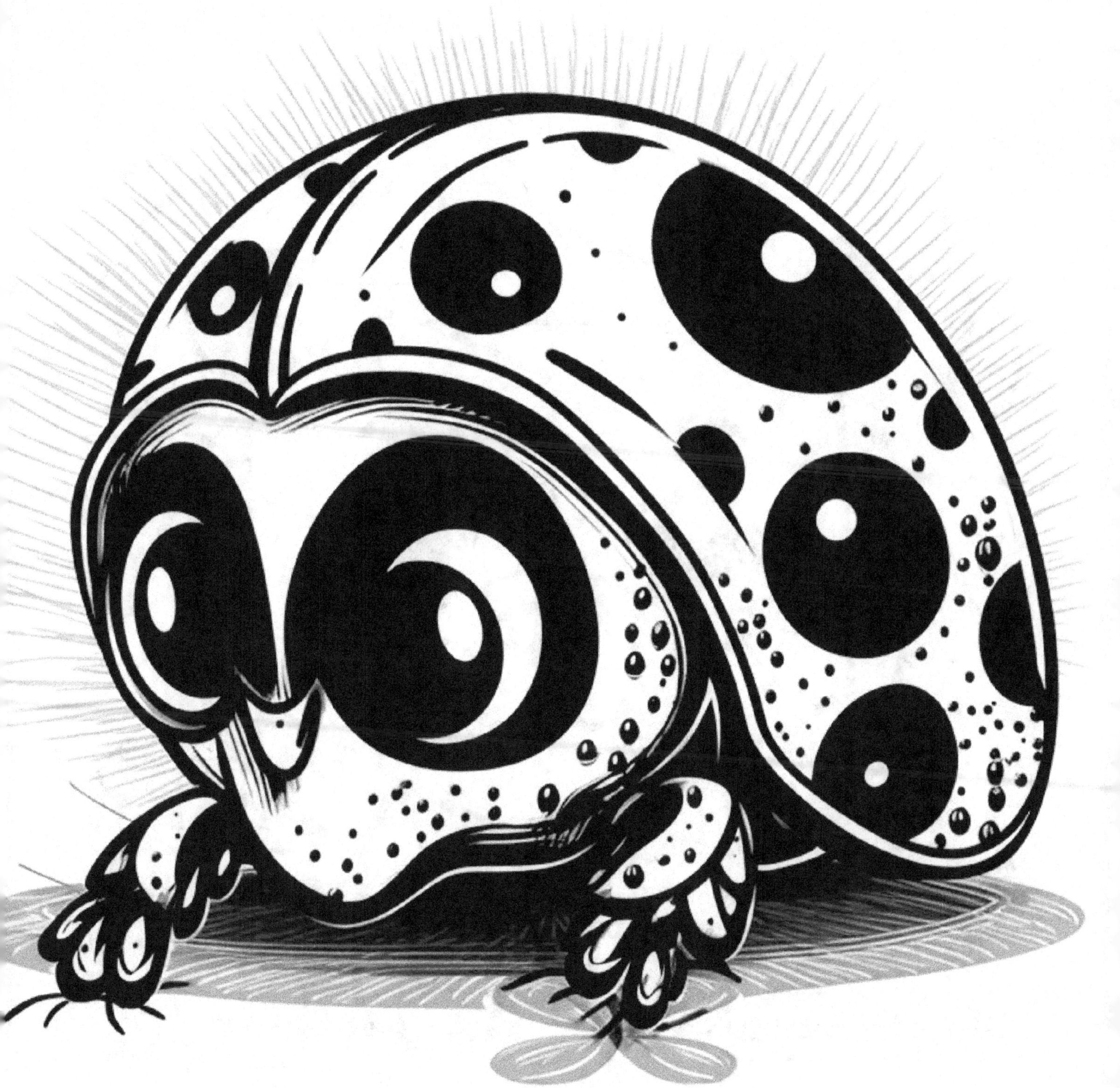

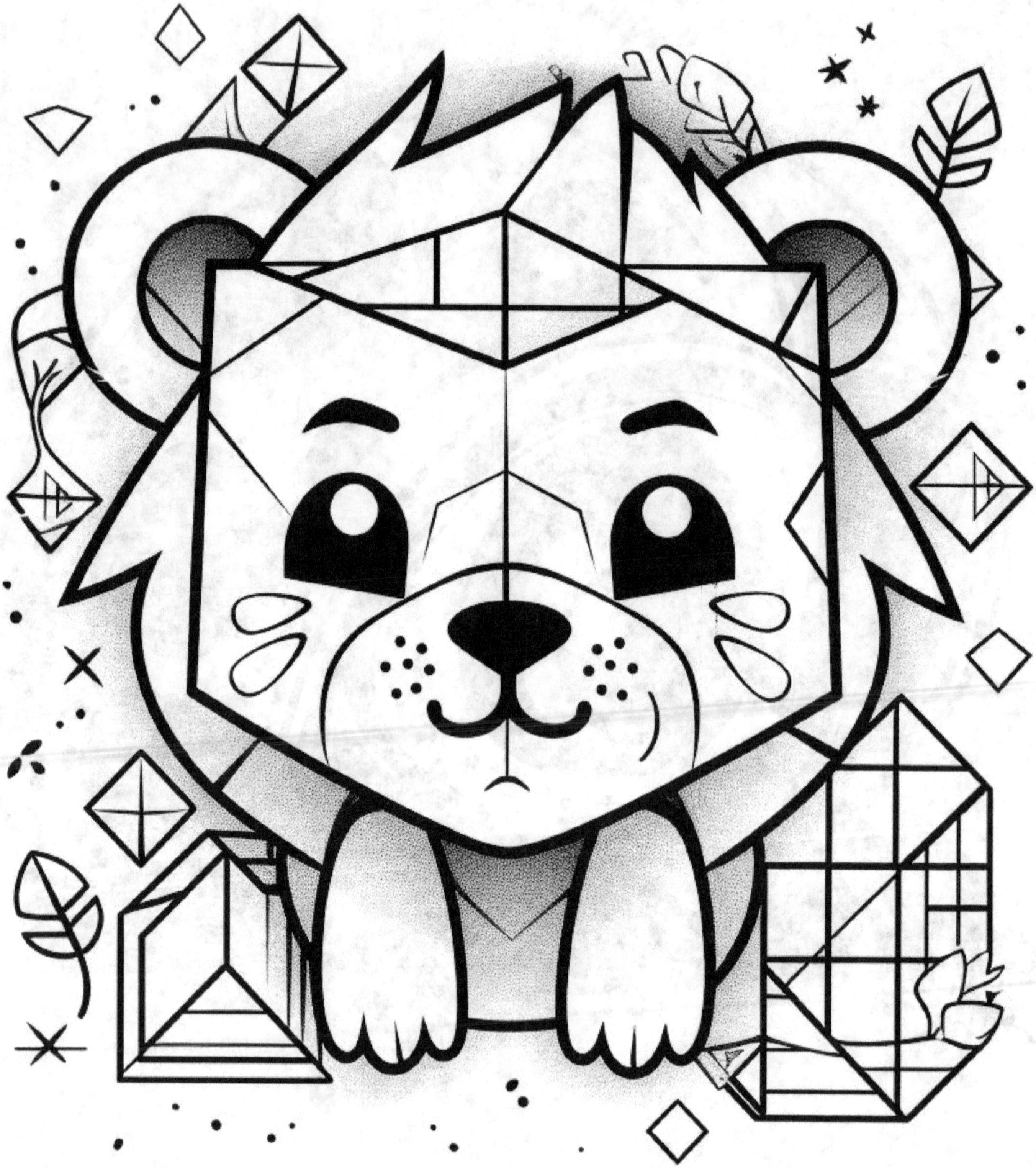

www.ingramcontent.com/pod-product-compliance
Lightning Source LLC
Chambersburg PA
CBHW080852220526
45467CB00008B/2483
* 9 7 9 8 3 9 2 6 2 2 3 8 2 *